# Living Landscape

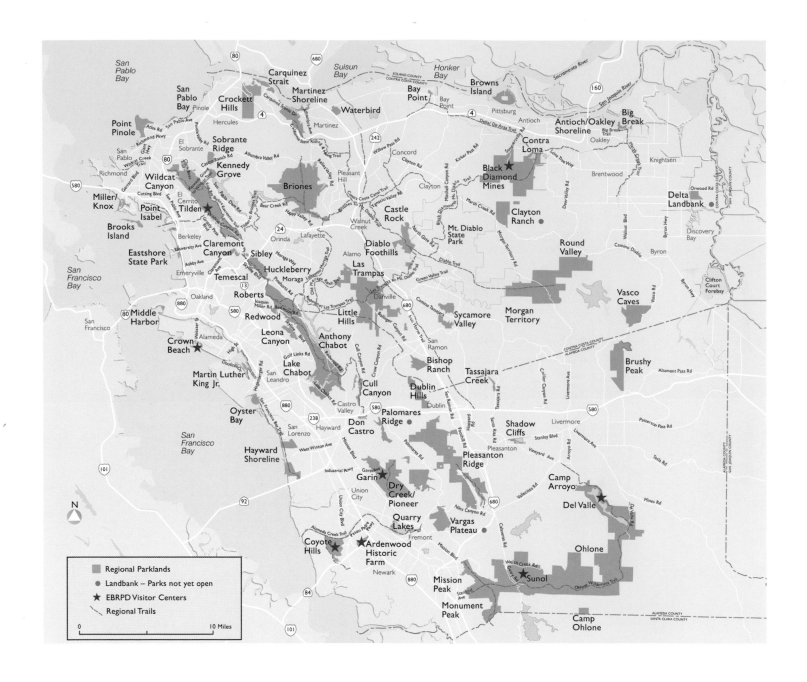

San Pablo Bay

San Pablo Bay

Suisun Bay

Honker Bay

SOLANO COUNTY
CONTRA COSTA COUNTY

Sacramento River

San Joaquin River

160

Carquinez Strait

Martinez Shoreline

Bay Point

Browns Island

Crockett Hills

Waterbird

Bay Point

Pittsburg

Antioch

Antioch/Oakley Shoreline

Big Break

Oakley

Knightsen

Point Pinole

San Pablo Bay

Pinole

Hercules

Sobrante Ridge

Kennedy Grove

Concord

Clayton Rd

Black Diamond Mines

Contra Loma

Clayton Ranch

Brentwood

Delta Landbank

Wildcat Canyon

Richmond

Briones

Pleasant Hill

Clayton

Castle Rock

Mt. Diablo State Park

Round Valley

Byron

Discovery Bay

Miller/Knox

El Cerrito

Point Isabel

Tilden

Walnut Creek

Diablo Foothills

Clifton Court Forebay

Brooks Island

Berkeley

Claremont Canyon

Orinda

Lafayette

Alamo

Las Trampas

Vasco Caves

Eastshore State Park

Sibley

Huckleberry

Morgan Territory

San Francisco Bay

Emeryville

Temescal

Moraga

Danville

Sycamore Valley

Roberts

Oakland

Little Hills

Middle Harbor

San Francisco

Redwood

Leona Canyon

Anthony Chabot

San Ramon

Bishop Ranch

CONTRA COSTA COUNTY
ALAMEDA COUNTY

Brushy Peak

Altamont Pass Rd

Crown Beach

Alameda

Lake Chabot

Tassajara Creek

Martin Luther King Jr.

San Leandro

Cull Canyon

Dublin Hills

Livermore

580

Patterson Pass Rd

Oyster Bay

Castro Valley

Don Castro

Dublin

Palomares Ridge

Shadow Cliffs

Pleasanton

Camp Arroyo

Hayward Shoreline

Hayward

Pleasanton Ridge

Del Valle

Garin

Union City

Dry Creek/Pioneer

Quarry Lakes

Vargas Plateau

Ohlone

Coyote Hills

Ardenwood Historic Farm

Fremont

Mission Peak

Newark

Sunol

Monument Peak

Camp Ohlone

ALAMEDA COUNTY
SANTA CLARA COUNTY

N

Regional Parklands

Landbank – Parks not yet open

EBRPD Visitor Centers

Regional Trails

0                    10 Miles

# Living Landscape

The extraordinary rise of the East Bay Regional Park District
and how it preserved 100,000 acres

Laura McCreery

**WILDERNESS PRESS** ... *on the trail since 1967*

**BERKELEY, CA**

Living Landscape: The extraordinary rise of the East Bay Regional Park District and
how it preserved 100,000 acres

**1st EDITION 2010**

Text copyright © 2010 by Laura McCreery

Front cover photo copyright © 2010 by Jason Armstrong
Interior photos credited on p. 186
Cover and book design: Suzanne Albertson
Book editors: Roslyn Bullas and Laura Shauger

ISBN 978-0-89997-628-0

Manufactured in China

Published by:  **Wilderness Press**
               **1345 8th Street**
               **Berkeley, CA 94710**
               **(800) 443-7227; FAX (510) 558-1696**
               **info@wildernesspress.com**
               **www.wildernesspress.com**

Visit our web site for a complete listing of our books and for ordering information.
Distributed by Publishers Group West

*Cover photo:* Round Valley Regional Preserve

**Library of Congress Cataloging-in-Publication Data**

McCreery, Laura.
    Living landscape : the extraordinary rise of the East Bay Regional Park District and how it preserved
100,000 acres / Laura McCreery.—1st ed.
        p. cm.
    Includes bibliographical references and index.
    ISBN 978-0-89997-628-0 (trade paper)
1.  East Bay Regional Park District (Calif.)—History. 2.  East Bay Regional Park District (Calif.)—
Environmental conditions. 3.  East Bay Region (Calif.)—History. 4.  East Bay Region (Calif.)—Environmental
conditions. 5.  Landscape—California—East Bay Region—History. 6.  Parks—California—East Bay Region—
History. 7.  Public lands—California—East Bay Region—History. 8.  Landscape protection—California—
East Bay Region—History. I. Title.
    F868.E22M35 2010
    979.4'65—dc22
                                                                                            2010004304

## A Note from the East Bay Regional Park District
### by General Manager Pat O'Brien

As we celebrate the 75th anniversary of the establishment of the East Bay Regional Park District, it gives me great pleasure to present this commemorative history. It's a remarkable story that I believe will be of interest to the public, the park district board, staff, and anyone who follows the workings of local government.

From its origin as a grassroots movement to preserve open space for public enjoyment, the East Bay Regional Park District has carried forward through the years with abundant public support to become the largest regional park agency in the U.S. The density of our population and the richness and variety of our natural landscape make this distinction all the more remarkable. A rare combination of voter confidence, public advocacy, and citizen participation has allowed the creation of East Bay regional parks and trails that reach into every corner of Alameda and Contra Costa counties, often side by side with the complex infrastructure of the urban zone.

Just recently the District added a parcel of land that allowed it to reach an important milestone: It now preserves and protects more than 100,000 acres of parks and open space in the public interest. I am proud to have been the District's general manager for the past twenty-one years, working with the elected board and a dedicated staff to make this achievement possible for the benefit of every East Bay resident.

On behalf of the board and staff, I would like to thank the author, Laura McCreery, for her work, and the public for its continuing support in the effort to preserve the natural beauty that has made the East Bay such an attractive place to live. Though a book of this modest length cannot cover every event of the last seventy-five years, we hope you enjoy this summary of our history.

A leaf-strewn path in Tilden Regional Park, one of the first three East Bay regional parks opened for public use in 1936. Originally named Wildcat Canyon Regional Park, it was later renamed to honor Major Charles Lee Tilden, one of the park district's first five board members upon its formation in 1934.

# Contents

Springtime view toward Mount Diablo from Briones Regional Park, one of the first two East Bay regional parks opened on former Contra Costa County lands (the other was Kennedy Grove Regional Recreation Area) after annexation of most of that county to the park district in 1964.

# Foreword

*by Congressman George Miller*

As a lifelong citizen of Contra Costa County, and its congressional representative over the past three decades, I have witnessed firsthand the East Bay Regional Park District's steady drive to protect open space and to build an impressive network of regional parks and shorelines. Though all the action while I was growing up was in neighboring Alameda County, most of my county joined the park district in 1964, when I was in college. I remember that annexation campaign, so I'm gratified by every piece of land and every new park added since then. Today I spend countless hours walking with my wife Cynthia in nearby Briones Regional Park. We and our two sons and five grandchildren can revel in the natural world just outside our door because of leadership by the park district's board and staff. The inside story of how they led—especially during the last twenty years—has not been told until now.

My father was a state senator when I was growing up in Martinez, and I learned from a young age the importance of working toward accomplishments that will live on for future generations. As a liberal Democrat who went to Sacramento with Adlai Stevenson's help and who founded the California Democratic Council and chaired the state Democratic Party, my father nevertheless worked across the aisle, as everyone did then, to accomplish things for all Californians. Though he was a close ally of Governor Pat Brown, he objected forcefully during the governor's 1958 reelection campaign to proposed increases in the transfer of delta water to Southern California. "He was rightly concerned that the pumps sucking away water for the south would cause incomprehensible environmental damage, not to mention the loss of water for local farming," wrote Brown biographer Ethan Rarick.

Because my father understood the interrelationship of local and state policies, his staunch support of the park district was a natural part of his commitment to constituents in our rapidly growing agricultural county. Although environmental protection was not yet in our vocabulary, and his strengths ran more to fiscal policy and labor relations anyway (he chaired the senate's powerful Finance Committee), he instilled in me and my three sisters a firm commitment to the environment that guides us to this day. Now it's a pleasure to read his name in these pages, along with the names of state legislators from both parties who represented our area, such as John Nejedly and Jack Knox. Dad would be especially gratified to know the park district has been in the hands of smart, assertive people who think like politicians and manage like financiers to advance the public good, just as he did.

My father died suddenly of a heart attack when he was only fifty-one and I was a law student of twenty-three. I sensed already that my life's work would in some way build upon his and my mother Dorothy's legacy of working for a more humane world. More than forty-five years later, I know the deep satisfaction of advocating for educational, labor, and environmental justice for all citizens.

Since being elected to Congress in 1974 on the heels of Watergate, I have aided the park district's work whenever possible as part of my personal commitment to protecting the environment and preserving open space. While chairing the House Natural Resources Committee from 1991 to 1994, I proudly sponsored and enacted a significant water reform law, the Central Valley Project Improvement Act of 1992. By involving the federal Bureau of Reclamation in managing the Central Valley Project, the act brought significant protection to the fish and wildlife of the San Francisco Bay and Delta region, where the park district also pursues active wildlife protection. As my father understood so well, water is an issue affecting all Californians at the local, state, and national levels of policymaking. I consider water reform among the most important milestones of my career.

While I pursued change through the Congress, the park district racked up impressive environmental successes at the regional level. Led by a dedicated board of directors and a strong general manager, Pat O'Brien, the agency grasped the rapid pace at which open space was disappearing. They stayed ahead of residential development in order to create more parks before it was too late, in some cases—such as Round Valley Regional Preserve in Contra Costa County or Claremont Canyon Regional Preserve in Alameda

County—exploiting or creating one-time opportunities to acquire lands that otherwise might never have come into public hands. By tracking every acre in the two counties, and by mastering every possible financial and legislative avenue, they pulled off a stunning expansion of parklands in the densely populated East Bay. As this book explains, such growth will never again be possible, as available land will soon be down to almost nothing. But because of the park district's sophisticated methods and expert implementation, we the people have nearby parks to pass on to our children and grandchildren.

*Living Landscape* takes the dry subject of management and finance and brings it alive through the eyes and views of those who made everything happen. We learn about the board and staff of the park district, but also about money, politics, and the environmental movement itself. As someone whose own adult life coincided with many of the events laid out here, I was transfixed by the story of how the agency acquired so much land on the public's behalf in Contra Costa County starting in the 1960s and how that work continues today in the changing world of land-use politics.

The book's portrait of financial changes after the passage of Proposition 13 in 1978 is an education for any Californian, revealing how the park district took on a creative advocacy role after property tax revenue shrank to a fraction of former levels. For the next thirty years the agency deftly set itself apart from other affected local governments, carefully financing both growth and existing operations during the boom times as well as the economic busts.

*Living Landscape* ensures that we won't take our regional parks for granted or forget how and why their history unfolded. As citizens of the East Bay and of California, we must never forget the courage and foresight of those who voted in November 1934 to create the East Bay Regional Park District for our benefit and for all future generations. As the poet Robert Frost said so aptly: "The land was ours before we were the land's."

U.S. Representative George Miller
Martinez, California

# Prologue

In the summer of 1988, as Americans prepared to elect either Vice President George H. W. Bush or Governor Michael Dukakis to the White House, the East Bay Regional Park District faced a momentous decision of its own. More than fifty years had passed since the District's founding in 1934, and a full ten years had elapsed since California voters had approved the sweeping tax revolt known as Proposition 13. Through careful stewardship the District had fared better than many local government agencies after Proposition 13 slashed property tax revenue, its main source of operating funds.

But recently the financial picture had taken a turn for the worse, and a watershed moment had now arrived. Should the District plan for a future that was, at best, merely satisfactory, or should it strive for the realm of the visionary?

The District's seven-member board of directors gathered to assess an idea launched only weeks before. Several directors supported the bold plan before them, but the president balked. As their debate carried from afternoon into evening, their hopes of agreeing began to fade. Their positions were too far apart, it seemed, their fundamental views of the risks too diverse. But when the matter was at last moved to a vote, the unthinkable occurred. The "ayes" had it.

The gamble was on: In the November 1988 general election the District would ask citizens of the East Bay counties of Alameda and Contra Costa to pass a massive $225 million capital bond measure. In keeping with its newly revised master plan, two years in the making, the District aimed to create 7,500 acres of new parks while enlarging existing parks by 20,000 acres. Fully 75 percent of bond funds would go to acquiring land and developing recreational facilities in the regional parks. The other 25 percent would provide capital grants to local park and recreation agencies within the two counties.

Achieving a two-thirds majority was a steep challenge for any ballot initiative, but this one, Measure AA, represented a financing structure that would make or break the District for the next twenty years. With nine statewide bond measures clamoring for funds on the same ballot—alongside twenty other nonfinancial statewide initiatives—voter approval might be out of reach.

As if the upcoming election were not challenge enough, the District also faced a wracking turmoil in its leadership. The general manager had just departed after a stormy tenure of only two-and-a-half years. Although the pace of land acquisition had increased during his administration, a corresponding debt stood unpaid and a sizable budget reserve was severely depleted. The details of day-to-day management had caused a sharp drop in employee morale, leaving many members of the administrative and field staff suspicious of the agency they loved and fearful about the future.

As the summer wore on, the board confronted the management situation and set about recruiting a new general manager. A promising, experienced candidate—one they had passed over three years before—now renewed their confidence and agreed to accept the top job. But he would arrive only after Measure AA was decided. With the election looming, individual members of the board grew agitated, knowing their own reputations were on the line.

Whatever the decision of voters, the District—long known as a model of innovation and creative leadership among large regional park agencies—would survive. But if Measure AA failed, would it thrive?

The two sons of Frederick Law Olmsted Sr., along with Ansel F. Hall of the National Park Service, surveyed potential East Bay parklands and recreational needs for the University of California, Berkeley's Bureau of Public Administration. The resulting Olmsted-Hall Report of 1930, "Proposed Park Reservations for East Bay Cities," became the blueprint for the East Bay Regional Park District and included this map of the proposed park.

# Chapter 1

# Beginnings

*The great variety of hill and valley, forest and plain, the absence of winter cold or summer heat, and the easy accessibility from all parts of the urban area brings to the fortunate people of the East Bay cities a continuous opportunity for the enjoyment of the great outdoors, under the most favorable conditions.*

—OLMSTED BROTHERS, landscape architects,
and ANSEL F. HALL of the National Park Service
"Proposed Park Reservations for East Bay Cities," 1930

Early on the evening of January 29, 1931, as a weak winter sun cast its final rays over San Francisco Bay, a few bundled figures began to assemble outside the grand exterior of the Hotel Oakland. Soon the line snaked around the corner of 13th Street and onto Harrison. Robert Gordon Sproul, president of the University of California, had once again rushed away from his family's evening meal to lend a ceremonial hand, this time with great personal interest as well. The moment he arrived, the doors were opened and East Bay citizens quickly filed in. But unlike the hordes that had so often entered to attend the luncheon meeting of a fraternal organization or in hopes of glimpsing President Herbert Hoover or Amelia Earhart, this crowd had a more ambitious purpose.

In spite of the Great Depression's devastating effects and the winter cold, these civic-minded citizens had assembled because they wished to create a park. Not a small park, but a 10,000-acre park that would stretch both north and south along the ridges of the East Bay hills.

President Sproul gave his opening remarks, and by the time park advocate Robert Sibley took the podium the crowd was more than a thousand strong. With every seat

Robert Gordon Sproul, president, University of California

taken, people spilled into the aisles and the nearby hall. Nevertheless they grew quiet as he called the meeting to order.

The idea of protecting wilderness by creating parks was not new. In fact, the notion of parklands in the East Bay had its roots in the nineteenth century. Frederick Law Olmsted Sr., the landscape architect for New York City's Central Park, had been invited in the 1860s to plan the University of California's flagship campus at Berkeley. Foreshadowing a key tenet of regional planning, he was among the first to articulate a human and aesthetic ideal of gardens in reach of cities. He suggested that "scenic lanes" be established over the oak-studded hills of Contra Costa County.

In the early twentieth century, two Oakland city planners in turn took up the cause of protecting "beautiful sites like Wildcat Canyon" in perpetuity for the benefit of all citizens. Nothing came of their urgings. In time, however, the fallow idea of East Bay parks was tilled again, like so many California stories, by controversy over the state's two great resources: land and water.

Since the 1860s, private water companies had bought up land and drilled wells to capitalize on the creeks and water table of the scenic Wildcat Canyon watershed. By damming canyons on these lands and storing the runoff in reservoirs such as Temescal and Chabot, many small suppliers provided water to a checkerboard of East Bay communities. By 1916, however, the inefficiencies of this system had given way to the consolidated East Bay Water Company.

A severe drought during and after World War I convinced East Bay residents that the ad hoc system of private "catchment" basins and reservoirs was no longer sufficient. After passage of enabling legislation by the State of California, they voted in May 1923 to form the East Bay Municipal Utility District, a "special district" for the counties of Alameda and Contra Costa. This public agency would build a new system to pipe water from the Mokelumne River in the Sierra Nevada.

The importance of a reliable water supply for the burgeoning East Bay region was thrown into sharp relief on September 17, 1923, when a grasslands fire ignited in Wildcat Canyon and—aided by hot, dry winds—raced west into Berkeley, consuming 640 structures, most of them homes, in a single day. The cause of the conflagration was never firmly identified, but the East Bay Water Company was roundly criticized for inadequate water delivery.

In 1928, five years after the successful water-district vote and the devastating fire, the new East Bay Municipal Utility District acquired the private water company and consolidated water service to the East Bay. Suddenly some 10,000 acres of former water-company lands, "twenty-two miles in length, extending [south to north] from the Chabot Reservoir at San Leandro to Richmond," were proclaimed surplus and available.

Although builders and developers showed considerable interest, local outdoor enthusiasts and civic leaders began exploring with city governments the possibility of creating parks instead. Such a result could be achieved two ways, either by amending the water district's charter to allow for management of parks or by forming a similar but separate agency of state government, a "special district" for parks alone. Pursuing the easiest solution first, an alliance of park and recreation groups petitioned the water district to set aside and administer 10,000 acres for parks. Citing a lack of authority to manage anything but public utilities, the directors refused.

In 1929, the same year the Mokelumne River began to supply water to the East Bay, several small park and recreation organizations joined to form the East Bay Regional Park Association. Robert Sibley, a University of California engineering professor and a stalwart of the California Alumni Association, was instrumental in adding leading citizens to the roster of members, which soon grew to 2,500.

When the stock market crash of October 1929 plunged the nation into economic turmoil, East Bay park advocates carried on undeterred. Sibley already had approached the Drury advertising agency to formulate an outreach campaign in support of converting former water-company lands into public parks. Aubrey Drury's response, delivered in November on six typewritten pages, included a plan to finance the effort with annual dues from park association memberships. Sibley wasted no time, and by early 1930 his efforts were under way.

At Sibley's suggestion, and aided by a grant from the Kahn Foundation, the Bureau of Public Administration at the University of California, Berkeley, commissioned the landscape architecture firm Olmsted Brothers (sons of Frederick Law Olmsted Sr.) and Ansel F. Hall of the National Park Service to survey the East Bay's recreational needs and available lands. The resulting Olmsted-Hall Report of 1930 envisioned along the East Bay hills a sizable park that would preserve land while stimulating recreational use. At only 900 existing park acres, the region lagged far behind other areas around the country for its geographic size and population. But without swift action, proposed parklands might go to private hands. If so, the report warned, the dire need for parks and open space might never be met.

"The East Bay communities face an unusual opportunity," the report concluded. "The present inadequacy of the region's park facilities . . . makes it apparent that an adequate portion of these publicly owned lands should be reserved for park purposes."

# Election Politics in California in 1934 and the New Deal Legacy

The general election of November 1934 capped a dramatic year in the history and politics of California, making voter approval of the East Bay Regional Park District all the more visionary for its unusual timing. Californians had already suffered five years of dire economic consequences of the Great Depression. The longshoremen's strike at the San Francisco waterfront in May gave way to a general strike in July that reverberated throughout the region and galvanized unions nationwide.

With the New Deal under way but unemployment still high and public assistance low, novelist Upton Sinclair ran for governor on a message of change. Although he pulled off an upset victory for the Democratic nomination in late August, the state's leading newspapers, including Harry Chandler's *Los Angeles Times,* the *San Francisco Examiner* and other papers of the William Randolph Hearst press, and Joseph Knowland's *Oakland Tribune* denounced him as a socialist who would threaten Americans' way of life. Earl Warren, then-district attorney for Alameda County—a position that later encompassed the District's first need for legal counsel—warned of impending Communism at the hands of Sinclair.

As Greg Mitchell wrote in *Editor and Publisher* before the November 2008 general election: "Sinclair, author of *The Jungle* and dozens of other muckraking books, had created a crisis not just for his home state but the entire nation by embracing FDR's New Deal while also leading a grassroots movement called EPIC (End Poverty in California) . . . . The prospect of a socialist governing the nation's most volatile state sparked nothing less than a revolution in American politics. With an assist from Hollywood, and leading newspapers, Sinclair's opponents virtually invented the modern media campaign . . . a stunning advance in the art of public relations." The Republican governor, Frank Merriam, won reelection, Mitchell observed, and only seventy-four years later did the *Los Angeles Times* for the first time endorse a Democrat, Barack Obama, for president.

After the successful 1934 election, the new District reaped the benefit of multiple projects by New Deal agencies such as the Works Progress Administration (WPA) and the Civilian Conservation Corps (CCC), including projects at Tilden Park's golf course and at Lake Anza. WPA workers also built Skyline Boulevard, linking the first string of parks in the hills above Berkeley and Oakland.

Historical geographer Gray Brechin and photographer Robert Dawson launched the Living New Deal Project in 2003 to document the New Deal's legacy in California through an online database (http://livingnewdeal.berkeley.edu) of facilities created or upgraded in those years. Writing in *Bay Nature* magazine in 2008, Brechin said: "CCC boys at Camp Strawberry Canyon produced ten large-scale relief maps of the East Bay to help win overwhelming voter approval for the creation of the East Bay Regional Park District in 1934."

Now, at the end of January 1931, Sibley's energetic vision had brought throngs of East Bay residents to the Hotel Oakland to set that report's vision in motion. By the time he adjourned the meeting and the crowd surged back into the streets, the East Bay Regional Park Association had its first thousand signatures on a petition to the water district. Another 13,000 residents would add their names, calling upon the water company to transform the 10,000 acres of surplus watershed land into a park and to amend its legislative charter to allow for park development and management for the counties of Alameda and Contra Costa.

Representatives of nine city governments in the two counties joined in petitioning the water district's directors. All but one, Chairman George Pardee, favored the change. "Persuasion went on for some time," and it appeared that Pardee, who had been California's governor from 1903 to 1907, might be won over. But his personality clash with park advocates—notably Major Charles Lee Tilden, an Alameda businessman and longtime rival—cemented his opposition, and he threatened to resign, convincing his fellow directors to veto the plan.

Pardee justified the decision in writing by emphasizing the "already onerous duties and responsibilities in administering a water system." He also cited financial concerns over some $3 million in outstanding bonds. Though the former governor was adamant that such issues could not be resolved, he was later said to regret his decision to cede control of the land and the corresponding water sources.

In spite of dissent from some of its own members about how to proceed, the East Bay Regional Park Association quickly shifted tactics, calling for creation of a new regional government agency to acquire and manage the proposed parklands. Mayors of the East Bay cities were supportive, and in 1933 the association instituted a semiofficial Regional Park Board chaired by Elbert Vail of the Oakland Planning Commission.

Never before had a state government attempted to form a "special district" to integrate preservation and recreation for the citizens of a fast-growing urban area. But Frank Mott, a former Oakland mayor now serving in the state assembly, drafted and successfully lobbied for a bill to authorize and establish just such a regional park "special district" for Alameda and Contra Costa counties and a governing board of five. Governor James Rolph signed the bill into law, the first of its kind in the nation. But one crucial task of forming the new park district—approval by the taxpayers—still lay ahead.

The East Bay Regional Park District's first logo, 1934

The East Bay Regional Park District's first board of directors confer with other park leaders. Standing from left to right are: August Vollmer, director; Nils Aanonsen, director, Works Progress Administration; Leroy R. Goodrich, director; Frank A. Kittredge, regional director, National Park Service; Roy C. Smith, inspector, National Park Service; Elbert M. Vail, general manager. Seated from left to right are: Thomas J. Roberts, director; John McLaren, designer, Golden Gate Park; Charles Lee Tilden, director and president; and Aurelia Henry Reinhardt, director.

An initiative appeared on the ballot in November 1934 to approve the new district and levy a tax of five cents on each $100 worth of property to finance the effort. The cities of El Cerrito and Richmond had to withdraw after Contra Costa County supervisors refused to authorize the election, but the ballot measure did enjoy the support of University of California President Robert Gordon Sproul—an early advocate for East Bay parks—and a host of civic leaders and organizations. Even in the depths of the Great Depression, citizens of seven cities in Alameda County voted 2½–1 in favor of the initiative, taxing themselves to create parks.

The new board of directors, elected on the same ballot, included Major Charles Lee Tilden, the Alameda businessman and Pardee opponent, who also chaired the Harbor Commission; labor leader Thomas J. "Tommy" Roberts; former Berkeley police chief August Vollmer; Dr. Aurelia Henry Reinhardt, the president of Mills College; and Leroy Goodrich, an Oakland attorney and port commissioner.

Within weeks of the election, the board printed a public statement of policy in local newspapers: "It will be our purpose to study and perfect a general plan to determine the lands to be acquired for park purposes, the manner of their development, and the work to be done. It will be our policy to insist upon the most rigid economy."

With that promise of fiscal restraint, the board looked again to the Oakland planning commissioner serving as the Regional Park Board's chairman, Elbert Vail, appointing him the first general manager of the new East Bay Regional Park District, without pay. He in turn hired his only staff member, Georgette Morton, as secretary and treasurer. After working briefly from Vail's planning commission office on Franklin Street in downtown Oakland, they established District headquarters in the nearby Bank of America Building at 12th and Broadway. The first priority was acquiring land, but negotiations with the water district proved complicated, and the two sides were far apart on price. The new District did buy 60 acres of privately held land in Redwood Canyon at $35 per acre.

By 1936 a compromise with the water district was reached. Alameda County's district attorney, Earl Warren, worked out a plan allowing the East Bay Regional Park District to purchase more than 2,000 acres at a little more than $300 an acre to form the first three parks, Wildcat Canyon (renamed Tilden Regional Park), Roundtop (now

Sibley Volcanic Regional Preserve), and Temescal (Regional Recreation Area). With this step, the new park agency accomplished a critical step in its development: eligibility for federal aid. In a spirit of great celebration, the board and staff held opening ceremonies in Oakland's Redwood Bowl in October 1936, inviting the public to enjoy the "people's playground."

General Manager Vail, now drawing a monthly salary of $300, laid plans to capitalize on one of the few benefits of the Great Depression: funds and workers from the New Deal agencies. The federal government would provide 60 percent of construction costs to develop the parks—mainly in worker salaries—while the District would furnish 40 percent, much of it surplus building materials from the construction of the Caldecott Tunnel connecting Oakland to Contra Costa County.

The next several years brought some $3 million in federal labor and materials, and soon the existing work camps in Wildcat Canyon hummed with Civilian Conservation Corps (CCC) and Works Progress Administration (WPA) projects. Local citizens were hired to construct Skyline Boulevard along the scenic ridge of the East Bay hills and to lay stones for a new headquarters building at Lake Temescal.

Using redwood and stone quarried in the parks, workers also built hostels, buildings, and amphitheaters. They created hiking trails, bridle paths, playing fields, and picnic grounds, and they dammed Wildcat Creek to create Lake Anza. Tilden Park quickly became an East Bay institution, with its championship golf course, botanic preserve, and the signature Brazil Building donated by the Brazilian government after the World's Fair on Treasure Island in 1939.

Meanwhile, the board and skeleton staff worked to buy nearly 1,500 additional water-district acres adjoining the 60 private acres previously acquired for Redwood Regional Park. Despite the effects of the Great Depression, General Manager Vail wrote the first long-range plan for the 1940s amid signs of real progress. The District now had

The East Bay Regional Park District's opening ceremony in Redwood Bowl on October 18, 1936, was an extravaganza featuring horses, archery, fencing, the University of California, Berkeley marching band, bagpipes, and military pageantry.

Works Progress Administration workers assemble for their day's assignment in Wildcat Canyon.

Director Tommy Roberts (left) helps Secretary Georgette Morton and General Manager Elbert Vail move into the East Bay Regional Park District's new headquarters building at Temescal.

Interpretive Specialist Jack Parker (left) describes a wildlife exhibit to General Manager Richard Walpole.

some 4,000 acres in four regional parks—Tilden, Roundtop (Sibley), Redwood, and Temescal—and more than a million users each year.

With the bombing of Pearl Harbor in December 1941, the District marshaled land and people for the war effort. The army conducted training in the parks and housed convalescing soldiers in the old CCC camps, while the Fourth Air Force established more than a dozen radar stations.

When Vail resigned as general manager in 1942 to go to Washington, D.C., the board chose Harold L. Curtiss of the U.S. Forest Service to replace him. Curtiss inherited a war footing, as the board had reduced the nickel tax rate to three cents, then again to two cents. The staff was shrinking as well. Wesley Adams, a former WPA worker, had been the District's first field employee in 1937.

"He was hired as a laborer when Tilden Park first opened," Georgette Morton recalled. "Then he was made superintendent out at Redwood Park because he showed an ability."

With the war raging abroad, Adams was now one of only six paid workers. He ran Redwood Park, even fighting its fires, with only the aid of his wife.

But with careful management the parks stayed open, and the District's finances held steady. By war's end, $300,000 in tax revenue had been invested in war savings bonds, and $200,000 more had accumulated in the general fund.

With the peace of 1945 came new leadership for the District. Richard Walpole had been hired away from the Los Angeles parks department in 1938 to build and manage Tilden Park's golf course. Prevented from joining the armed services by Governor Earl Warren, who named him to head the East Bay Fire Protective Association, Walpole was now the board's choice to become general manager.

In 1946 the board restored the full nickel tax rate and expanded plans for recreational amenities. The Tilden Merry-Go-Round, a vintage carousel built in 1911, was dedicated in 1948—the first in the East Bay—followed by the pony ride, the steam train, and a trout pond. The board also set aside funds to purchase war surplus trucks, trailers, and tractors, along with two old airport crash vehicles that served as fire trucks.

The business of land acquisition resumed. New parcels increased the size of Redwood Park, and an 88-acre adjacent area was purchased in 1951 and transformed into Roberts Regional Recreation Area in honor of board member and union leader Tommy Roberts.

Turning again to the water district, the East Bay Regional Park District in 1953 negotiated purchase of nearly 3,000 acres of the scenic Grass Valley in southern Alameda County (later christened Anthony Chabot Regional Park in recognition of the engineer who dammed Lake Chabot).

By its 20th anniversary in 1954, the District had 5,400 acres, a budget of $652,000, 47 full-time and 43 seasonal or part-time employees, and 2.7 million annual visitors. Residents of nearby Eden and Washington townships voted, in 1956 and 1958 respectively, to annex themselves to the District, broadening the tax base at a critical time. General Manager Walpole had built up a surplus to buy land, and when he retired citing poor health in 1960, he left his interim successor, Wesley Adams, in strong financial shape.

The arrival of William Penn Mott Jr. as general manager in 1962 signaled a period of vigorous growth and change for the East Bay Regional Park District. Trained as a landscape architect, Mott had begun his career supervising Depression-era public works projects for the National Park Service.

As superintendent of parks for the City of Oakland starting in 1945, he had proven himself a creative and energetic leader. Oakland became the first city in the nation to hire a naturalist for public education and the first to create a concession for youngsters, Children's Fairyland. Mott also became adept, even evangelical, at lobbying for his projects, inspiring both admiration and envy among the city administrators who had to compete with him for funds.

"This ability to squeeze water out of a rock ... puts Mott in a class by himself," said a local pundit in 1947.

Purchased from the East Bay Municipal Utility District for $225,000 and opened in 1952, Grass Valley represented more than 950 acres of new parkland serving equestrians and other users in the vicinity of Oakland, San Leandro, Hayward, and Castro Valley. The park was later named Anthony Chabot Regional Park after the engineer who dammed Lake Chabot in the nineteenth century.

Acting General Manager Wes Adams (on right, with shovel) and a group of staff and board members pose at the groundbreaking ceremony for the East Bay Regional Park District's new headquarters building on Skyline Boulevard in Oakland.

The District's board of directors continued to attract exceptional leaders, including Dr. Robert Gordon Sproul, president emeritus of the University of California. In 1960 Sproul suggested Mott as the District's next general manager. His four colleagues on the board were enthusiastic, but Mott would not consider a change until he had completed a major renovation of Oakland parks. Sensing that Mott was worth waiting for, the board held the job open, and after two years Sproul made the proposal again. This time Mott accepted.

Once hired, Mott applied the vigorous style he had developed in Oakland to his work with the District, reorganizing the administrative structure, hiring expert departmental managers, acquiring substantial new lands, and planning for long-range growth.

Some staff members, accustomed to General Manager Walpole's hands-off informality, were taken aback by their new leader. Mott "wanted to know what you did and how you did it," said one longtime employee.

"He insisted on excellence," said another. "He didn't just mouth it—he demanded it."

While Mott maintained high standards for his managers and staff, he also displayed a genuinely friendly interest in all employees, often stopping his District car without warning to introduce himself to someone digging a ditch or trimming a tree. "Good morning. I'm Bill Mott," he would say. "How are things going?"

Mott combined a personal touch with strong support of the union. He agreed that, for the first time, employees could use a checkoff to deduct dues from their paychecks. Having held blue-collar jobs himself, he had a strong sense of fairness and an equally strong drive to build loyalty.

While Mott's relations with employees generally were good, he occasionally aroused strong opposition. When he decided in 1965 to move the botanic garden from Tilden to a larger space at Anthony Chabot Regional Park—and to shed the garden's longtime supervisor, James Roof, in the process—a group calling itself the Friends of the Tilden Park Botanic Garden rallied behind Roof and convinced the board to reverse the plan. Rather than disband after the botanic-garden campaign, the group reinvented itself as the California Native Plant Society.

Assessing the District's public offerings, Mott reviewed the small but effective interpretive program, which focused mainly on Junior Rangers, and transformed it into a comprehensive department under the leadership of Chris Nelson, whom he hired away from the Sacramento Junior Museum. "He wanted the most innovative, creative interpretive program ever devised," Nelson said later.

As for financing new parks, General Manager Mott needed revenue to buy land before it was scooped up by developers. With key aid from state legislators, the District passed a bill in 1963 authorizing a temporary five-cent "override" of property tax rates solely for land acquisition and capital improvements. The capital spending limits were lifted in 1967, and by 1971 the additional five-cent tax was permanent, bringing the total tax rate for parks to ten cents per $100 of property value.

General Manager William Penn Mott Jr. visits a day camp for Girl Scouts at Sunol Regional Wilderness.

A capstone of Mott's tenure was his leadership in annexing western and central Contra Costa County to the District. Although a county park department existed there, it had no operating parks, as voters had several times rejected bond funding. With the help of a strong campaign committee, Mott and his new public information director, Richard "Dick" C. Trudeau, persuaded 54 percent of voters to pass the 1964 annexation ballot measure. The easternmost Liberty township excluded itself under the sway of asparagus farmers there, but the annexation represented an enormous change in much of the semirural county.

As county counsel and district attorney for Contra Costa, John Nejedly was instrumental in bringing the two counties together. "We kept pushing this idea of collective management," he said. "It was a basic feeling that the two counties could do a far better job working together." The county board of supervisors was a particularly tough sell, as annexation meant a new taxing district that they did not control. "That was not a politically attractive idea," Nejedly recalled, "but I just kept working on them."

Through that campaign Trudeau also made the acquaintance of the Contra Costa Park and Recreation Council president, Hulet Hornbeck, whose career would soon entwine with his own. "Hulet had very good knowledge of [Contra Costa] county," Trudeau recalled.

The growing tax base in these new areas of Contra Costa helped, and the District expanded further with the annexation of Pleasanton in southern Alameda County in 1966. In contrast to the campaign for Contra Costa, the ballot measure for the Pleasanton area enjoyed strong support, including that of the *Pleasanton Times,* and an astounding 80 percent of voters gave their approval.

With the county counsel, Nejedly, as liaison to the legislature, Mott moved quickly to expand the District's landholdings, converting former Contra Costa County lands into Kennedy Grove Regional Recreation Area and Briones Regional Park. With funding from a 1965 state bond issue, he guided the acquisition of Las Trampas Regional Wilderness near Danville, also in Contra Costa County, and Coyote Hills Regional Park in southern Alameda County.

"Coyote Hills was the big one, and that's the one that the [bond] money went to," Trudeau recalled.

Several years of negotiations for the nearly 3,000-acre Sunol Regional Wilderness in southern Alameda County also bore fruit. (With later additions, Sunol approaches 7,000 acres today.)

With land acquisition a top priority, Mott interviewed three candidates and hired Hulet Hornbeck as the District's first chief of land acquisition.

"Hulet was an interesting person to work with," Trudeau said later. "He was a stormy petrel when he came in." Although Hornbeck did not openly disagree with Mott, Trudeau said, "He did actually in a lot of ways." But Hornbeck's intimate knowledge of both land and owners went a long way, and his partnership with Mott got results.

Mott himself believed strongly in recreation as a counterpart to preservation. While adding considerable acreage to the District, he also pursued new and improved facilities for camping, picnicking, swimming, riding, and hiking. After rebuilding beaches at Lake Anza and Lake Temescal, he and the California Anglers Association convinced the East Bay Municipal Utility District to grant the first public access to a reservoir, Lake Chabot, which opened with a fishing derby in 1966.

Meanwhile, the District was eyeing the shoreline as a fitting counterpart to its inland parks and freshwater recreation sites. When Save the Bay (founded as the Save San Francisco Bay Association) and the newly formed Bay Conservation and Development Commission waged a grassroots campaign to halt both the filling of the bay and the elimination of marshlands, the District joined in and laid plans to acquire waterfront parks.

The first such shoreline, Alameda State Beach, had been turned over to District management by the City of Alameda in 1967. Its transformation to Crown Memorial State

The view from Crown Memorial State Beach in Alameda takes in the San Francisco skyline in the background.

Beach took fifteen years and was fraught with erosion problems, but in time it became the busiest swimming beach on San Francisco Bay.

But in 1967, just when many of Mott's efforts were succeeding, the District took an unexpected hit. Governor Ronald Reagan too had taken notice of Mott's skills and was now luring him away to Sacramento to direct the California Department of Parks and Recreation.

Suddenly the District's "Mott era" was over, but in five short years Mott had more than doubled landholdings from 7,400 acres to more than 17,000. Twenty parks in two counties now served three times as many visitors as before, and the annual budget was nearly $12 million. The board and staff looked ahead with apprehension. Without Mott at the helm, how could the challenges of booming population and land development, combined with steady inflation, be met?

The hills and valleys of Apperson Ridge, adjacent to the Sunol Regional Wilderness, would have been altered forever if quarrying had been allowed to proceed.

## Chapter 2

# Expansion

*As the flat lands of the Bay Area have been covered by urbanization, most of these grass covered, rolling hills have survived largely unspoiled, providing a scenic counterpoint to the urban area. Green during the winter and spring, golden brown in the summer and fall, the Ridgelands afford visual and psychological relief from the often frantic pace of life in the urban area.*

—"Ridgelands: A Multijurisdictional Open Space Study," 1977, published by Alameda, Contra Costa, and Santa Clara counties, the East Bay Regional Park District, the Association of Bay Area Governments, and the Bureau of Outdoor Recreation

For some time after his departure in 1967, the question of who would replace William Penn Mott as general manager weighed upon the directors of the East Bay Regional Park District. By promoting Mott's planning and design chief, Irwin Luckman, they assured a smooth transition to a known leader. Like Mott, Luckman had trained as an architect. After five years at the helm of planning and design, his artistic vision now graced many District properties. He had created the first inner swimming lagoon fed by a reservoir at Cull Canyon Regional Recreation Area, winning a 1966 Governor's Design Award. His own interest in the environment kept him involved in such organizations as People for Open Space. But he soon decided he was a poor match for the job of administrator, and he resigned after only a year.

William Penn Mott Jr. (left) at Cull Canyon Regional Recreation Area with planning and design chief Irwin Luckman, who succeeded him in 1967 as general manager of the East Bay Regional Park District

Landscape architect Irwin Luckman, the East Bay Regional Park District's planning and design chief, created the award-winning swimming lagoon at Cull Canyon Regional Recreation Area.

The board quickly promoted public relations director Richard "Dick" C. Trudeau to acting general manager. In 1969, after a national search—and at the urging of state senator George Miller—the board voted 5–2 to make Trudeau's appointment permanent.

"I'd been 'acting' long enough that the staff got used to working with me," Trudeau said later, "... and I was doing reasonably well at it, if I say so myself."

Trudeau had been a public relations man from a tender age. As a tall, energetic youngster impaired by ear and eye problems, he had been forced to come to terms with a limited physical capacity for sports. But his love of athletics pushed him instead to promote sports teams and events. In prep school, high school, and at the University of Washington, he emphasized journalism and political science, running many political campaigns and special events with flair. Always his love of the outdoors was voiced clearly and practiced often.

After graduate study in public administration and a two-year stint in Denmark with the U.S. Department of State, Trudeau pursued a career with nonprofit organizations, developing many personal and business contacts in the East Bay and at the state capital in Sacramento. When Mott hired him to develop legislative and public relations for the District in 1962, the two had known one another for more than ten years through the United Way of the Bay Area.

By the time of his promotion in 1968, Trudeau's savvy tenure as head of public relations had strengthened the District's relationships in local communities and in the state legislature. As acting general manager, he soon faced tests of his capacity for leadership. When the widespread social unrest of 1968 flared up in East Bay communities, he formed a partnership with the City of Oakland to bring youngsters to nearby Roberts and Redwood parks for swimming, picnics, and team sports.

For the delta communities at the northern edge of Contra Costa County, Trudeau pushed to create Contra Loma Regional Park at a federal reservoir in only six weeks so the youths of Pittsburg and Antioch would have nearby recreation for the hot summer months. After the park's opening in 1968, the *New York Times* carried a short history of the surrounding area, once the site of boomtowns for Welsh coal miners. The sparkling new facilities of Contra Loma now stood nearby, the article noted, charging no user fees except fifty cents for parking. "The park is free for youngsters who come on foot or by bicycle, as they do in droves."

That article brought national recognition to the District's efforts to establish parks in underserved areas. Along with swimming, boating, and fishing, Contra Loma evolved to offer 776 acres of land leased from the U.S. Bureau of Reclamation for hiking, riding, picnicking, and field sports. Like the surrounding area, the park also provided habitat for myriad mammals, including coyotes, gray foxes, and deer.

For Trudeau and his staff, bigger challenges now loomed. Adjacent to Sunol Regional Wilderness near the District's southern border, the basalt and rock atop Apperson Ridge was threatened with removal by Utah Construction and Mining Company.

General Manger Dick Trudeau (left) and Nobel laureate Glenn Seaborg

Lacking only a zoning variance from Alameda County supervisors, Utah planned to quarry the ridge over the course of a thirty-year lease.

The District objected outright, then sought compromise. When Utah refused, the District waged a yearlong campaign to convince county supervisors to deny the permit. Supervisor Joe Bort played a critical role in the eventual decision to side with the District, with a vote of 4–1.

The *Oakland Tribune* later quoted Trudeau on the subject of seeking common ground between park advocates and developers: "I know we're doing the job when both sides are mad at us," he said. This theme of warring adversaries would run throughout his tenure.

Under Trudeau's direction the District diligently pursued such urgent matters as Apperson Ridge while also setting priorities for land acquisition that would double the thirty-four square miles of parks now managed. To fund these ambitious plans, the board voted to seek an unprecedented ten-cent tax increase from the state legislature. Assemblyman Jack Knox agreed to sponsor the measure if the state's legislative analyst deemed the plan sound and if key business interests supported it.

Again Trudeau teamed up with Supervisor Joe Bort of Alameda County, who agreed to chair the campaign. Together they collaborated with Senator John Nejedly on a distribution ratio for the proposed tax increase: Seven cents out of every ten would go to land acquisition and three cents to development of parklands for public use.

"I guess we spent about a year lobbying and getting support," Bort recalled. "Then one of the most amazing things—that I couldn't possibly have imagined—was that the Sierra Club opposed the bill."

Bort never knew the specific reason for the local Sierra Club opposition, but the chapter had a history of pressing hard for land preservation while actively opposing development. By taking the matter to the Sierra Club's state chapter, Trudeau and Bort in time got the endorsement they sought. In return they agreed to increase the ratio of land acquisition from seven to eight cents out of every ten while scaling back development to only two cents.

After systematic building of grassroots and legislative support, the Knox bill passed in 1971. It was the only tax increase signed by Governor Ronald Reagan that year. Trudeau's sense of victory was boundless, but in typical fashion he gave credit to a slew of others whose efforts were critical, especially Joe Bort and Bill Mott—now director of state parks—and state legislators Nejedly, Nicholas Petris, Dan Boatwright, and, of course, the bill's sponsor, Knox.

---

Stewart Udall, former secretary of the U.S. Department of the Interior and principal of the technical consulting firm Overview, Inc., speaking at a public hearing about the East Bay Regional Park District's master planning process

With the tax bill signed, the District faced more hard work. The first five-cent rate increase would occur right away in 1972, but the second only after a new master plan had been adopted. Although the District had engaged in long-range planning for years, this master-plan mandate was different. Armed with federal funds awarded through the Association of Bay Area Governments, the District staff worked with professional planners, citizen advisers, and local governments to establish criteria, methods, plans, and maps for evaluating possible land acquisitions.

By designating each parcel a regional park, recreation area, wilderness, shoreline park, trail, preserve, or land bank, planners included a wide variety of lands with good geographic distribution based on population and assessed value.

The District took the unprecedented step of contracting with former Interior Secretary Stewart Udall's planning firm, Overview, Inc., to facilitate the technical aspects. Twenty-one public hearings took place across the two-county territory, and two large public advisory committees helped establish community priorities.

Today exceeding 3,000 acres, Garin Regional Park in the Hayward hills (shown here with Mission Peak in the distance) looks much as it did throughout its cattle ranching history.

The resulting master plan, revised several times since its adoption in 1974, resulted in a balanced and much larger system of parks. As an added benefit, the two public advisory committees evolved into a single permanent Park Advisory Committee with members appointed by the District board from its own nominations as well as those of public agencies in both counties.

With a key goal of expanding public access to the waterfront—in concert with Save the Bay, the Audubon Society, the Bay Conservation and Development Commission, and the Coastal Conservancy—the District continued the work of establishing shoreline parks along the eastern edge of San Francisco Bay, beginning with the long process of creating Crown Memorial State Beach and acquiring Point Pinole.

On higher ground, Trudeau and his land acquisition chief, Hulet Hornbeck, teamed up to acquire and open other lands for public use, such as Mission Peak in the southern reaches of Alameda County; and in Contra Costa County the Black Diamond Mines

# Open Space Studies

**1966** The Association of Bay Area Governments (ABAG), an association of Bay Area city and county governments formed in 1961, published a preliminary regional plan designating eight categories of "permanent" open space, also proposing that 1.6 million acres be designated "open space for urban expansion" by 1990.

**1968** People for Open Space published "The Case for Open Space" to explore and test the financial feasibility of ABAG's 1966 plan.

**1977** In "Ridgelands: A Multijurisdictional Open Space Study," Alameda, Contra Costa, and Santa Clara counties, the East Bay Regional Park District, ABAG, and the Bureau of Outdoor Recreation set forth recommendations for planning, urban development, land acquisition, and management.

**1980** The National Park Service studied the idea of establishing a national park in the East Bay. Although it found no need for federal protection in the region, it called on local governments to form a permanent ridgeland-protection organization. Congressman Don Edwards introduced a bill in 1981 (cosponsored by Ron Dellums, George Miller, and Pete Stark), but the bill failed and a regional coordination program never materialized.

**1991** The Greenbelt Alliance published "The Bay Area's Farmlands," a report documenting "the region's vibrant but still fragile agriculture."

**2000** The Greenbelt Alliance published "At Risk: The Bay Area Greenbelt," concluding that nearly 500,000 greenbelt acres could be paved in the next thirty years.

**2002** The Bay Area Open Space Council's "Diablo Ridgelands Working Group," a voluntary partnership of nonprofit land-management organizations and public agencies, released "The Diablo Ridgelands: Protecting and Enhancing a Regional Landscape," setting forth threats to Diablo ridgelands in relation to broad land-use planning matters.

**2003** The Greenbelt Alliance analyzed Contra Costa County's growth and land-use history in "Contra Costa County: Smart Growth or Sprawl?"

**2006** The Greenbelt Alliance published a new edition of its 2000 landmark study, "At Risk: The Bay Area Greenbelt," identifying 401,500 acres of greenbelt lands at risk of sprawl development.

**2009** The Bay Area Open Space Council and Greenbelt Alliance released "Golden Lands, Golden Opportunity: Preserving Vital Bay Area Lands for All Californians," a two-year collaborative review of challenges to and strategies for protecting open space in the nine-county San Francisco Bay Area. The report set forth three key actions for the future: create access, fund conservation, and adopt strong policies.

Regional Preserve, Diablo Foothills Regional Park, and Morgan Territory Regional Preserve.

While building the size and scope of District properties, General Manager Trudeau also transformed many business practices. He introduced a new method of calculating the budget and placed a greater emphasis on planning, commissioning the District's first studies of citizen satisfaction and economic benefits. For employees, he emphasized formal job descriptions and goal setting, and he instituted professional management of construction projects. Faced with increased demands for public safety and fire prevention in the growing park system, he made it a top priority to assure adequate resources for those functions.

Interpretive programs evolved significantly at Ardenwood, Coyote Hills, and Crab Cove and at the "pioneer parks" Garin and Dry Creek, where the public could learn first-hand about traditional methods of farming, ranching, and blacksmithing. At Black Diamond Mines, the interpretive staff guided visitors through California's largest coal mine.

In 1974 the board commissioned a management study that resulted in a development and training program. Meanwhile, the District became an early adopter of an affirmative action program in 1973, setting formal goals for ethnic and gender parity in employment.

But a labor strike in 1975—the only one in District history—was a sober reminder that fast growth and dramatic change did not come easily. The management study had recommended that managers and supervisors be placed outside the union, and the District now aimed to remove about forty such employees from union ranks. Many of the affected individuals reported negative or mixed views of the change, and the strike persisted for more than two months.

The parks stayed open during the dispute with only eighteen top management employees and the public safety department on duty, and in time a compromise was reached. Park supervisors stayed in the union, while some park managers joined the management team, including "zone managers" who would oversee the District's widely dispersed field operations.

———————————

Despite such rough spots, the District was well on the way to fulfilling many aspects of its master plan. But the passage in June 1978 of Proposition 13, the statewide property tax revolt, brought an abrupt halt. Like all public agencies, the District now faced a threat to its very financial existence.

The morning after the election, General Manager Trudeau addressed a conference of the California Park & Recreation Society, acknowledging the harsh realities of Proposition 13 but also urging his listeners to respond creatively. "Out of defeat can come victory," he insisted.

Faced with the loss of more than 50 percent of tax revenue, Trudeau and his staff reduced operating expenses for 1979 by $1 million, while working aggressively to find other sources of funds. Despite their efforts, 20 percent of the District's employees would have to go.

"The hardest part that I had to do was cutting people off the staff," Trudeau said. He wrote to employees at home asking for suggestions. Out of 200 employees, he said, "I got a hundred letters back with ideas. Some of them were very good."

Trudeau let newcomers go first and then consolidated other administrative and field staff. Through it all, he refused to reduce the department of public safety or the naturalists, who at Bill Mott's suggestion were now working directly with schools to teach children about the natural world. One innovation growing directly out of Proposition 13 was Adopt-a-Park, a program matching corporate sponsors with parks needing labor and outright funding.

"You can get corporations to [support charitable agencies] if they see that it's worth doing and valuable to the public," Trudeau said. "There was no reason, then, why we shouldn't get the same thing happening for parks."

Kaiser Aluminum was the first to adopt, choosing Roberts Recreation Area in Oakland. The Clorox Company followed suit at Coyote Hills Regional Park near Newark. In time the Regional Parks Foundation, a Trudeau innovation in existence since 1969, took over Adopt-a-Park and also expanded the pursuit of local charitable and business grants to help fill the gaping hole left by Proposition 13.

In the late sixties, Trudeau had taken Assemblyman Jack Knox's advice to improve the District's legal representation. After interviewing three firms, Trudeau and the board selected Orr, Wendel & Lawlor to replace the Alameda County Counsel's office as legal counsel. Principal Clayton Orr advised many a land acquisition, a role later assumed by his successor, Donn Black. Now, in the wake of Proposition 13, Trudeau saw the need for professional representation in Sacramento as well. He tapped John Zierold, lobbyist for the Sierra Club, and together they pushed to add "stopgap" funding for the District to a state assembly package.

The bill passed: For the first time offshore oil money in the state Energy and Resources Fund would be used for parks as well as schools. Yet again, Trudeau's creative touch and carefully tended connections in state government, along with the hard work of his staff, had set the District apart from comparable agencies.

The District regained a decent financial footing, but the time had come to make the master plan consistent with the realities of Proposition 13. A revision, adopted in 1980, called for development of less than 10 percent of park holdings and protection of the other 90 percent in their natural condition.

"The District shall have as one of its primary goals the equitable distribution of regional parklands to create a balanced system of both existing and new parklands, designed to reflect the needs and desires of all District residents," the plan stated.

As liaison with Sacramento took on added significance and the District's lobbyist decided to concentrate his efforts with the Sierra Club, Trudeau and the board sought new representation. Director Ted Radke led a search and strongly recommended, against Trudeau's preference, that Ternes and Houston serve as the new lobbying firm. Bob Houston, and later his son Doug, proved highly effective.

"We've used Ternes and Houston since 1980, and they have been great," Radke said.

Considering the changes wrought by Proposition 13, the District's overall outlook was good. Since its inception as California's first special district devoted to parklands, the East Bay Regional Park District had formed and nurtured an integrated system of land acquisition, restoration, management, and preservation. With the long-sought annexation of eastern Contra Costa County, accomplished in 1981, the geographically diverse two-county service area was nearly complete, lacking only the greater Livermore area of Alameda County.

Over its first half century, the District repeatedly expanded its holdings of parklands, all the while adapting to dramatic shifts in economics, demographics, and social needs. By 1984, the fiftieth anniversary, the resulting network of parks approached 60,000 acres, serving millions of visitors each year from the dense urban population of the Bay Area. That, by any measure, was something to be proud of. But even after the seemingly impossible hurdles and the rousing successes of the first fifty years, some of the most dramatic moments were yet to come.

## Regional Parks Foundation

This 2004 photo captures an East Bay Regional Park District day camp at Martin Luther King Jr. Regional Shoreline in Oakland. The camp is one of many sponsored each year by the Regional Parks Foundation's campership program.

Like many influential institutions, the Regional Parks Foundation got its start in an unexpected way. When Kaiser Sand and Gravel completed a years-long quarrying operation on land it owned in southern Alameda County, officials wished to donate the land to the East Bay Regional Park District so it could be transformed into a public park. Company bylaws, however, prevented direct donation to a public agency.

Rather than accept that fate, then-General Manager Dick Trudeau got creative. He conceived a private nonprofit entity that would exist to advocate for and financially support the District. Incorporated in 1969 as a nonprofit entity under section 501(c)(3) of the IRS code, the Regional Parks Foundation stood alone as the first park-related entity of its kind in the U.S.

Kaiser Sand and Gravel donated the land to the new entity, which immediately transferred the same parcel to the District. The District used the property value as a match for federal Land and Water Conservation Fund grant funds. Planning and design chief Lew Crutcher went to work on a unique park concept, and the federal grant supported initial development of what is now Shadow Cliffs Regional Recreation Area near Pleasanton.

"That was an innovative solution with a great public benefit and an auspicious beginning for the Regional Parks Foundation," said the foundation's executive director, Rosemary Cameron.

Governed by a committed volunteer board of directors, the foundation attracts participation from major corporations in the East Bay, as well as the banking, financial management, real estate, and law sectors. The board has played an essential role in raising more than $40 million over the life of the foundation.

One key service that evolved under Cameron's direction is the "seeding" of volunteer campaigns in support of the District's own ballot measures and other statewide initiatives.

"The foundation has the legal authority and flexibility to accomplish things that cannot be done by public agencies," Cameron said. "The foundation board has been able to designate nearly a half million dollars of its unrestricted funds toward ballot campaigns benefiting the District over the years."

Board members, appointed to two-year terms on a rotating basis (no more than four consecutive terms), also work closely with Cameron on core initiatives:

- **Campership**, a top-priority program that has sent thousands of low-income, at-risk, and disabled youngsters to both summer day camping programs as well as Camp Arroyo's weeklong environmental education program.

- **Parks Express**, a low-cost transportation program allowing organized groups to bring underrepresented populations of children and adults, especially senior citizens, into the regional parks.

- **Environmental Restoration**, a program supporting habitat restoration within the regional parks for grasslands and for a variety of threatened bird and amphibian species.

- **Membership**, a program offering individual and family members—more than 7,000 of them—special benefits such as free parking and swimming to make the regional parks even more accessible.

- **Planned Giving**, a program offering financial and estate planning to individuals and families wishing to make legacy donations to help preserve and improve the regional parks in years to come.

REGIONAL
PARKS
FOUNDATION

At more than 5,000 acres, the Las Trampas Regional Wilderness in Contra Costa County offers a variety of landscapes and microclimates, as well as unparalleled views of Mount Diablo.

## Chapter 3

# Land

*A regional open space program would not impose a major financial burden on Bay Area residents … even the most costly technique—complete purchase of all Bay Area open space lands—would cost no more than $10 per person per year.*

—"The Case for Open Space,"
summary of study by People for Open Space, 1969

Even before Hulet Hornbeck hired on as the East Bay Regional Park District's first land acquisition chief in 1965, he knew what he wanted most of all to accomplish there. At first, though, he kept his goal to himself.

A native of New Jersey who grew up poor in Newark and in Detroit, he had studied forestry at the University of Maine and then taken a law degree at Rutgers on the GI Bill. When his East Coast bond firm transferred him to San Francisco in 1957, he traversed the financial world by day but made his home in Contra Costa County, quickly falling in love with the open Western landscape.

As president of the Contra Costa Park and Recreation Council since 1959, Hornbeck had championed the nascent county park agency only to see the failure of multiple bond measures that would have funded actual parks.

When the District in 1964 tried again to annex Contra Costa to its existing Alameda County territory—thereby fulfilling its mission as a two-county regional park "special district"—he was instrumental in helping General Manager William Penn Mott and PR director Dick Trudeau pull the annexation off.

Through his park council advocacy, he had worked to build relationships with leaders in local government and in agriculture, the area's primary

This cartoon appeared in several small newspapers in Contra Costa County before the election in which Measure B passed to annex Contra Costa County to the East Bay Regional Park District.

business sector. Although small cities hugged the base of 3,849-foot Mount Diablo—the county's exceptional geographic feature—as well as the East Bay hills and the alluvial plain bordering the inland delta, most of the land consisted of privately owned open space: cattle ranches, walnut orchards, and other large-scale agricultural enterprises.

Talking with constituents about preserving open space by creating parks was a delicate matter that required both knowledge and diplomacy. Hornbeck had both.

When a doctor diagnosed a melanoma in 1965 and gave Hornbeck five years to live, he underwent surgery and began thinking in earnest about what was important to him. He was hardly out of his bathrobe—"I may still have been in my bathrobe"—when he showed up at Bill Mott's house.

"I want to work for you," he told Mott.

The District had three openings, including one in land acquisition, and Hornbeck applied for all of them. He was forty-six years old.

Soon, selected by Mott from among fifty applicants to implement an ambitious land program, Hornbeck was charged with looking into the future and staying ahead of the curve of residential development.

John Nejedly (left), district attorney and county counsel for Contra Costa County, and Hulet Hornbeck of the Contra Costa Park and Recreation Council display a map of the planned Briones Regional Park.

"When you're buying land for parks, you have to look ahead twenty-five years," Mott said later. In Contra Costa, he added, "We were thinking in terms of what was going to happen when this whole area mushroomed."

Contra Costa's population did grow by more than one-third between 1960 and 1970. Soon more than a half million people were in need of parks. With a ready supply of cheap land, willing sellers, and state bond funding earmarked for parks, the sky was the limit, at least in principle.

Alameda County, the District's other half, had a million residents in about the same land area (738 square miles compared to Contra Costa's 720), but it was not growing nearly so fast.

Already Hornbeck had aided Mott in his drive to create Contra Costa's first two regional parks at Briones and Kennedy Grove, both on former water district lands owned by the county.

Wearing the new hat of land chief, he launched an aggressive push for more land, quickly adding significant acreage to Briones and purchasing initial sections that would become other regional parks.

Hornbeck also joined Mott to acquire Coyote Hills Regional Park in southern Alameda County with funds from the 1964 state park bond act.

The golden hills of Briones Regional Park in Contra Costa County

Coyote Hills Regional Park in southern Alameda County

Although the county had designated bond funds for that purpose, the District found itself in competition with the Hayward Area Recreation and Park District.

Not realizing anyone from East Bay regional parks was present, a Hayward representative spoke against the District at a hearing of the state parks department. But Hornbeck identified himself and was asked to respond.

"If Bill Mott says he can build a park down there for these kinds of monies, the East Bay Regional Park District can do it," he said.

With that, the vote was his.

Even with that hurdle cleared, Coyote Hills proved a complicated acquisition. In time the District filed a condemnation on the property, but Hornbeck worked closely with the multigenerational family owners and built a solid relationship that saw all parties through a long and difficult process.

"If there is a parcel of land that is essential for the park . . . or for making the park usable, and if you cannot acquire it by negotiation, you then have to condemn the property," Hornbeck said. "The power is called eminent domain . . . and it is given to the District by the State of California legislature."

At Coyote Hills, as elsewhere, the basic authority to condemn—which often brings a tax advantage to the owner—made an essential difference in outcome. Without that option, the District could provide far fewer parks to its citizens.

Hornbeck also worked at Mott's side to acquire in 1966 the first section of the remote Las Trampas property in Contra Costa County. Later he would be instrumental in adding substantial acreage to the park from multiple private owners. His creative touch helped the National Park Service establish a national historic site at Tao House, the playwright Eugene O'Neill's former home.

"We bought the land and we had this [year-and-a-half option to buy] the home," Hornbeck said.

Transferring the option to a citizens' group working to preserve the site, the District helped create a unique arrangement for the federal government to own and manage the home, even though it sat in the midst of the vast oak and bay laurel woodlands of Las Trampas Regional Wilderness.

"That's an example of the option process working," Hornbeck said.

Drawing upon his own friendships for the frequent Contra Costa acquisitions, Hornbeck got in the habit of working with John Nejedly, the district attorney and county counsel who was the key to getting support from both the county board of supervisors and the state legislature.

"He was smart enough to figure out how to manage me," Nejedly said.

When Nejedly was elected to the state senate in 1969, he replaced the late George Miller as the regular carrier of the District's legislation there. Jack Knox often filled the same role in the assembly.

By then Hornbeck had refined his method to a fine art, and both legislators received many visits from him.

"He would always show up at the house, and he'd always give me the sad story, 'We know it can't be done, but they asked me to talk to you anyway,'" Nejedly said. "By the time he'd get through wringing the tears out of the towels, I would agree."

Dick Trudeau had succeeded Mott as the District's general manager by then, and he was pushing to expand the number and size of parks. Although Trudeau lacked Mott's larger-than-life charisma, he was so skilled at putting others to work for his cause that his extroverted style came across as powerful and smooth.

Hornbeck was a near-perfect foil. Understated, even taciturn, he "kept a low public profile, barking 'no comment' to news reporters asking about land deals."

Together, Trudeau and Hornbeck made a formidable financial team as well. In addition to seizing upon the series of state bond acts for which the District was eligible (passed in 1964, 1974, 1976, and 1980), they looked to new federal programs of President Lyndon B. Johnson's administration, especially the Land and Water Conservation Fund and the Title VII matching grant program of the Department of Housing and Urban Development.

"Every one of our acquisitions from 1965 through 1971 was made with funds matched either by a federal or a state grant," Hornbeck recalled. "For a number of those land acquisitions, the state money was matched by a federal grant and the cost to this District was nominal."

The Johnson administration also proved a critical backdrop for that important matter Hornbeck had been keeping to himself since his arrival. He thought about it every day while working to acquire parklands for the East Bay. Though it was no longer really a secret, he knew enough about human nature to bide his time and seek the proper conditions before saying too much.

Now it was time to say aloud what he wanted most to work on in his new career, and he could say it in a single word—trails.

George Cardinet (holding horse reins) of the State Horsemen's Association celebrating a statewide trail event

The District had, of course, been in the trail business throughout its history. All regional parks except those in land bank status had at least minimal trails, many converted from fire access routes or old ranching roads. Several active hiking clubs, such as the Contra Costa Hills Club, predated the District itself and had been instrumental in helping to realize the first regional parks in the 1930s. Mott, too, had pushed the concept of an interconnecting system of trails around the bay, but realization of that vision would take many years.

Hornbeck himself was a trail user from way back. Having hiked in New York and New Jersey as a youngster, he arrived in California eager to explore the scenic pleasures of the West.

"The very first thing I did was join the Sierra Club," he said.

His years with the Contra Costa Park and Recreation Council had been centered on getting parks, so trails were not much discussed. He noticed, though, that when parks finally began to materialize in Contra Costa, people did want trails.

"I realized that the hikers and the equestrians were constantly fighting each other," Hornbeck recalled.

Teaming up with George Cardinet of the State Horsemen's Association, he decided to put all interested parties in the same room with a mandate to find common ground.

The resulting East Bay Area Trails Council met monthly, also sponsoring picnics and field trips to keep all sides working together.

Meanwhile, President Johnson in 1968 signed the National Trails System Act, giving new status to the concept of a national trail system. When 100 volunteers and federal agency representatives gathered for the first national symposium on trails in June 1971, Hornbeck returned home from Washington, D.C., with an even greater fire in his belly to link East Bay regional park trails to other local and national trails.

## East Bay and Regional Trail Systems

The East Bay Regional Park District offers more than 1,150 miles of trails within its borders, including segments of the San Francisco Bay Trail and the Bay Area Ridge Trail.

**Alameda Creek Regional Trail** (11 miles east to west in southern Alameda County) follows the banks of Alameda Creek from the mouth of Niles Canyon in Fremont to San Francisco Bay, with access to Coyote Hills Regional Park. Opened in 1973, the trail received partial funding from the U.S. Army Corps of Engineers and the Alameda County Flood Control and Water Conservation District.

**Bay Area Ridge Trail** (projected 550-mile trail circling the ridges near San Francisco and San Pablo bays) exists for use by hikers, equestrians, cyclists, and others and includes significant segments within District lands, from Crockett Hills and Wildcat Canyon in the north to the southern boundary near Mission Peak. For more information, visit www.ridgetrail.org.

**Briones to Mount Diablo Regional Trail** (12 miles west to east in central Contra Costa County) connects Briones Regional Park with Mount Diablo State Park, providing both paved and unpaved trails—including a wheelchair-accessible section—near Lafayette and Walnut Creek (with connections to several other regional trails).

**California State Riding and Hiking Trail** (projected 22-mile Contra Costa County segment of statewide trail system). Under development since 1945, this project included the Contra Costa segment—from Martinez southeast to Mount Diablo State Park—as a pilot project. Senator Dan Boatwright led the effort to secure $300,000 in state funding from 1964 state park bond funds. After intermittent progress over many years, the District in 2009 set the goal of constructing a new segment in Concord.

**Contra Costa Canal Regional Trail** (14 miles in central Contra Costa County) offers a multi-use, accessible paved pathway following the arc of the Contra Costa Canal from Martinez through Pleasant Hill and Walnut Creek to Concord. Suitable for walkers, bikers, and runners, it was created in cooperation with the Contra Costa Water District and the U.S. Bureau of Reclamation, which began constructing the canal itself in the 1930s for crop irrigation, completing the job after World War II.

**Delta de Anza Regional Trail** (projected at 25 miles in eastern Contra Costa County) is named for a route taken by Spanish explorer Juan Bautista de Anza in the eighteenth century. This paved, multi-use hiking, bicycling, and equestrian trail (mostly wheelchair accessible) connects Concord, Bay Point, Pittsburg, Antioch, and Oakley, providing access to Contra Loma Regional Park and Black Diamond Mines Regional Preserve.

**Iron Horse Regional Trail** (projected 52 miles at completion, from Suisun Bay in Contra Costa County to Altamont Pass in southeast Alameda County) provides a wide, multiuse, whole-access trail

Aerial view of the Iron Horse Regional Trail

tracing the Southern Pacific Railroad right-of-way established in 1891 and abandoned in 1977. Created through cooperative efforts by agencies, individuals, and community groups, it offers both recreational and commute access, connecting residential communities with commercial areas, schools, public transportation, parks, and other regional trails.

**Lafayette-Moraga Regional Trail** (8-mile linear park) parallels St. Mary's Road, connecting Las Trampas Ridge to the Oakland Hills, Lafayette, and Moraga. Once used by mule trains to carry redwood lumber from Oakland to Sacramento, the route later carried lumber by steam train and then served as a utility easement before being established as a recreational trail serving hikers, cyclists, and equestrians.

**Marsh Creek Trail** (projected 14 miles at completion in eastern Contra Costa County) is a paved, flat, multiuse trail along Marsh Creek that ultimately connects the Delta region with Morgan Territory and Round Valley regional preserves.

**San Francisco Bay Trail** (projected 500-mile trail circling San Francisco and San Pablo bays) was created by Bill Lockyer's legislation in the state senate and passed into law in 1987. This recreational corridor, planned by the Association of Bay Area Governments, provides a shoreline network of trails for the nine Bay Area counties, connecting to public transportation and passing through urban areas and remote natural areas alike. In keeping with policies to protect sensitive natural habitats, the project includes paved paths, dirt trails, and bike lanes and routes. Individual trail segments are built, owned, and maintained by cities, counties, park districts, and other land-management agencies, often in partnership with local organizations and businesses. For more information such as maps and newsletters, visit the trail's web site, http://baytrail.abag.ca.gov.

A second meeting in Chicago in 1972 established the National Trails Council to push state and federal governments to coordinate their efforts. With Hornbeck as a founding member, the District would take a leadership role on a national scale, while continuing to give priority to trails within its own boundaries.

With the backing of Senator Nejedly in Sacramento, Hornbeck collaborated again with George Cardinet to seek funding and engage in strategic planning for trails. Cardinet was an old hand, a voice for equestrian trails since the 1940s when work had begun on creating a system of state riding and hiking trails. Cardinet was the source of many ideas about California trails, sort of a visionary "godfather of cross-state, cross-county, cross-city trails," and Hornbeck now played the complementary role of advocate and implementer.

Working closely with the District's planning manager, Lew Crutcher, Cardinet and Hornbeck began to tackle the prickly matter of rights and easements from private landowners, public utilities, and flood control districts. By the end of 1975, segments had been purchased or easements granted for the Alameda Creek Trail, the Contra Costa Canal Trail, and a section of the Skyline National Trail. Many more trails were in the works or at least in the plans.

## California Environmental Quality Act of 1970

The California Environmental Quality Act (CEQA) is a state statute that was enacted in 1970, shortly after passage of the federal National Environmental Policy Act (NEPA) in 1969. In response to the federal law, the state assembly created the Assembly Select Committee on Environmental Quality to study the possibility of supplementing NEPA through state law. The committee's report, "The Environmental Bill of Rights," recommended creation of a California counterpart to NEPA. As a result the legislature passed, and Governor Ronald Reagan signed, the CEQA statute.

The principal author of CEQA, Assemblyman John "Jack" T. Knox, had help shaping the law from a young environmentalist in his assembly district, Ted Radke, who later served on the Martinez City Council and the East Bay Regional Park District board of directors. Knox remained a great advocate for the District and for the environment, and the Miller/Knox Regional Shoreline bore his name when it opened in 1977 (along with that of his late colleague in the state legislature, Senator George Miller).

Codified in the California Public Resources Code (Section 21000 et seq.), CEQA requires state and local agencies (1) to identify significant environmental impacts of proposed development, including submission of environmental impact reports (EIRs) in advance, if required, and (2) to avoid or mitigate those impacts where possible.

Within the District's own board of directors and staff, the trails concept drew some opposition. After all, what business had they to become involved with trails outside their park borders, even outside their overall territory? Even with funds in hand to acquire trails, Hornbeck found, the going was slow.

———————————

Passage in 1970 of the California Environmental Quality Act added another dimension to many aspects of the District's planning and land acquisition functions, and as the trails project developed alongside the booming land program, the environmental impact reports kept piling up. Crutcher would need help to review these and make recommendations.

A young ranger at the newly opened Black Diamond Mines Regional Preserve had come to Crutcher's attention at a board of supervisors meeting and now crossed his mind again. As a founding member while still in high school of the environmental group Save Mount Diablo, Robert "Bob" E. Doyle had been mentored by Dr. Mary Bowerman, whose 1944 book on the flowering plants of Mount Diablo still reigns as a classic, and by Art Bonwell, who taught him to think at the intersection of science and ecology. These and other "wise old owls" of Save Mount Diablo opened up a world of ideas and advocacy on behalf of the natural world.

While soaking up concepts, Doyle had embraced the wilderness experience as well. An avid hiker, he had jumped at the chance to reside seasonally in Mount Diablo State Park, living for a time in a cabin on the mountain's remote east side and authoring the Mount Diablo Interpretive Association's first trail map of the park. While studying biogeography at San Francisco State College, he had been brought into the District, first on a volunteer trail crew and then as a seasonal ranger, by legendary park supervisor Walter Knight. Hired back full-time at Point Pinole Regional Shoreline and later at Black Diamond, Doyle had added field skills to his toolbox, everything from identifying wildflowers

The hills of Black Diamond Mines Regional Preserve (Contra Costa County) with a view of Rose Hill Cemetery (center): Although little remains of the nineteenth-century coal mining communities that once existed nearby, the Protestant burial ground serves as a monument to former residents (many from Welsh mining families but also of other nationalities) who died in mining disasters, epidemics, or childbirth, as well as from other causes.

to wielding chain saws. Crutcher put the young ranger to work, and in less than a year the environmental impact reports had been tamed. Doyle intended to return to Black Diamond, but Hornbeck had other ideas.

"We want to keep you here," he said. "Would you be interested in being in charge of the regional trails program?"

Now Doyle began his land career in earnest, working closely with Hornbeck on trails and, in time, on everything else. They, too, made a good team. With Trudeau at their back, there was little they could not accomplish once their minds were set.

As their operation grew in scope and sophistication, the District's master plan continued to provide a solid framework on which to base site selection.

"Many master plans or general plans are simply documents on a shelf," Hornbeck said. "This is one of implementation. It just works beautifully."

In keeping with the plan's emphasis on "balanced parkland," Hornbeck tried to think ahead and stay active in all parts of the two-county territory.

"I tried to keep them all going so that no given geographical area got too far ahead of the others," he said.

"A great majority of our acquisitions, though they were pragmatic in the sense of time, were not pragmatic in the sense of location," he added. "The location was selected on the basis of merit, and the time was chosen at the best interest of the property owner."

In addition to the long process of adding to Wildcat Canyon Regional Park, created from City of Richmond lands and dozens of other privately held parcels, the land team brokered Western Electric's dedication of 300 acres that would form the majority of Bishop Ranch Regional Preserve, in central Contra Costa County, at no land cost.

"Western Electric intended to sell all excess holdings to developers until the idea was floated of a portion being preserved as a park," Doyle said later. "This was the first land dedication in Contra Costa tied to residential development."

At times, citizen advocates made the initial push to create a new park. In the heart of Alameda County, for example, amid one of the densest population centers in the nation, board members Mary Jefferds and Harlan Kessel joined other activists to mount a massive campaign to preserve the steep and dramatic Claremont Canyon.

As they expected, such a difficult urban acquisition was not an easy commitment for the District to make. Only after they pressed hard—browbeat, even—to win support from the full board and the staff could the District begin the years-long process of piecing together a regional park from private lands abutting the University of California, Berkeley.

In keeping with his own legal training and strategic methods, Hornbeck had already scoured the country for the best land attorney he could find, Jack Rogers, and brought him in to support staff efforts. Together they tackled the long list of land parcels the new park would require, using the law as needed to get results. Although one parcel came in at twenty-eight acres and another at sixty-four, nearly 300 other private parcels were painstakingly acquired less than an acre at a time. Even with a court-ordered blanket condemnation, several tiny pieces—at only five- to eight-hundredths of an acre—involved just as much effort and liaison with owners as the sizable parcels that characterized the District's purchases elsewhere.

As the new park began to take shape, Assemblyman Tom Bates carried legislation to acquire from the State of California a crucial eighty acres—the former grounds of the school for the deaf—in exchange for land at the base of Mount Diablo, a trade that would expand the state park there.

It seemed the work would never cease, but at last the patchwork of properties was stitched together and Claremont Canyon Regional Park stood whole, an unqualified jewel. Just steps away from the crush of urban life, citizens now could dip in and out of the canyon's fragrant woodlands to scale the ridgetop and savor a stunning bay view in the company of raptors.

As Jefferds phrased it, "Come, look down on a soaring hawk."

The steep and spectacular Claremont Canyon Regional Park (Alameda County), shown here in the foreground, was pieced together from more than 300 small private parcels over the course of more than twenty years. This west-facing image includes the East Bay's urban landscape, San Francisco Bay, and San Francisco itself.

———————

Having perfected the role of citizen advocate himself, Hornbeck could play every part demanded by the drama of a new park. Riding shotgun with General Manager Trudeau, he nearly always achieved what he set out to do for parks.

By the time he retired in 1985 after twenty years as land chief—having the time of his life every day—he had helped Mott and Trudeau acquire 50,000 acres of parklands in both counties, adding new parks to the system and greatly expanding existing ones. And to his everlasting delight, nearly 100 miles of regional trails crisscrossed the District's two-county area, solid evidence of a dream fulfilled.

His melanoma had never returned.

This peaceful and majestic redwood grove is just a few miles from downtown Oakland, in Redwood Regional Park. The park's 1,829 acres also include chaparral and grasslands and Redwood Creek, where the world famous rainbow trout were first identified as a distinct species.

## Chapter 4

# Leadership

*One of the major themes in California history since at least the progressive era has been controversy over the use and preservation of the state's natural resources . . . . The struggle between the forces of economic development and environmental protection was waged on many fronts.*

—JAMES J. RAWLS and WALTON BEAN,
*California: An Interpretive History,* 1998

The national economic recession of the early 1980s wreaked a particular havoc on the State of California. When a new governor, George Deukmejian, took office in 1983, he faced a $1.5 billion budget deficit and a state unemployment rate exceeding 11 percent. After five years of property tax cuts imposed by Proposition 13, local government entities were raising fees and slashing services with abandon.

Against this backdrop, the East Bay Regional Park District was holding its own. At the helm since 1968, Richard "Dick" C. Trudeau had presided over significant expansion and preservation of open spaces for Alameda and Contra Costa Counties, swelling the number of regional parks from nineteen to forty-five and the total land area from 17,000 acres to more than 60,000. His steely determination, tempered with a philosophy of compromise and a knack for bringing opposites together, put the District at the cutting edge of park management and kept staff members hopping to fulfill the ambitions of their leader.

In the outside world, the District's board of directors, administrative philosophy, stewardship methods, and effective government liaison aroused interest and imitation from park agencies nationwide. Trudeau's success at fundraising led directly and indirectly to millions in state bonds and other public and private funds, much of it keeping the District afloat after the devastating effects of Proposition 13. Formation of the Regional Parks Foundation, the first park-affiliated nonprofit in the nation, was but one of his financial and programmatic innovations.

The District's constituents in the two counties gave resounding support to their system of parks. A telephone survey conducted by an outside firm, Tyler Research Associates, in 1976 reported 62 percent of adult residents "very satisfied" with their parks and another 32 percent "somewhat satisfied."

Inside the organization, Trudeau enjoyed many solid personal and professional relationships. Ever the PR man, he acknowledged and praised his staff often, sharing credit for every success with them, both collectively and individually by name. Years later his land acquisitions chief, Hulet Hornbeck, called it "a wonderful experience" to work for him.

"You didn't have to be a yes-man with Dick Trudeau," he said. "All you had to do is tell him what the facts were and where we were going. He'd back you to the end of the world as long as the direction was honest."

In spite of Trudeau's clear and continuing success, his management-by-crisis style was taking a personal toll. After the protracted second phase of negotiations to prevent a quarry operation from altering Apperson Ridge, near the Sunol Regional Wilderness, his fierce energy began to flag.

Relations between Trudeau and individual board members, sometimes edgy over the years, now too often crossed into the realm of hostile. At times, even on important matters, they were openly at odds. With a seven-member board, four votes could pass anything, and Trudeau had become a master of the four-vote victory.

"It was a very split board," said Jerry Kent, who had long served as Trudeau's deputy. "There were 3–4 votes on a whole lot of issues, and on Dick himself it was likely 3–4."

Within the board's own ranks, tension had long existed between environmental protection, on the one hand, and, on the other, public access to recreation facilities and programs in the parks. With roots in the Sierra Club, the Audubon Society, and other environmental protection organizations, some park directors liked the idea of having a general manager whose sensibilities more closely matched their own.

In the mold of Bill Mott, Trudeau was, by contrast, a professional park and recreation advocate and administrator. An environmentalist in his own right, he was nonetheless oriented toward creating and managing parks that citizens could actually use. Protecting open space was an important thing, as evidenced in the master plan and in many land acquisitions he brokered, but it was not the only thing.

If pressure existed to remove Dick Trudeau and replace him with a strict environmentalist, it was not overt. After all, nothing was black and white. History had shown that even the staunchest open space advocate might take a favorable position on recreation services for citizens of his own jurisdiction, whereas those supporting greater public access might also go to great lengths to protect open space.

Whatever the hue of this natural complexity, one thing became increasingly clear. Trudeau had worn himself down. If he retired, at least some of the directors would gladly replace him. With his key goals realized and his influence on the board eroded, Trudeau took stock of his options. In the spring of 1985 he announced his retirement from the job he had lived and breathed for seventeen years.

The board of directors of the East Bay Regional Park District in 1986: (from left) John O'Donnell, Jim Duncan, Mary Jefferds, Harlan Kessel, Lynn Bowers, Kathryn Petersen, and Ted Radke

"He was a fighter," Kent said later. "Parks didn't happen by accident. You had to fight for them."

Before Trudeau departed on June 30, 1985, the District's directors set about finding his replacement. Kent, the District's longtime assistant general manager—now serving as acting general manager—was a popular leader but did not want the top job.

"The board wanted a change in direction," Kent said. "They were looking for a different kind of general manager to reshape Trudeau's team."

---

The board enlisted a consultant to narrow a large pool of applicants from around the country to a shorter list of candidates. Among them were several park professionals from eastern states and Pat O'Brien, general manager of Southgate Recreation and Park District in Sacramento, who was asked by Trudeau to apply.

Director Harlan Kessel solicited and actively championed his own candidate for the job. Mary Jefferds joined with Kessel and, lobbying their fellow park directors, they advanced David E. Pesonen to a series of interviews. At their behest, and with testimonials from assembly speaker Willie Brown and other legislators, the board appointed him general manager in July on a vote of 6–1.

David Pesonen, general manager of the East Bay Regional Park District from September 1985 through March 1988

Pesonen, an attorney who also held a degree in forestry, had come into the public eye while working at UC Berkeley's Agricultural Experiment Station in 1960. While writing a report on recreation resources, he received a letter from "the dean of Western writers," Wallace Stegner. That document, known today simply as "the wilderness letter," was a thirteen-paragraph call to action that became a blueprint for much of the environmental movement in California and the West. Stegner had by then penned seven novels and several works of nonfiction, including *Beyond the Hundredth Meridian*, his biography of geologist-explorer John Wesley Powell.

Upon hearing of Pesonen's pending recreation report, Stegner wrote to "urge some arguments for wilderness preservation that involve recreation, as it is ordinarily conceived, hardly at all."

"What I want to speak for is not so much the wilderness uses, valuable as those are, but the wilderness idea, which is a resource in itself," Stegner wrote.

"Something will have gone out of us as a people if we ever let the remaining wilderness be destroyed," he added. "Just as surely as [progress] has brought us increased comfort and more material goods, it has brought us spiritual losses."

As the sixties unfolded, Pesonen stepped up his legal work related to the environment, helping to avert Pacific Gas & Electric's construction of a nuclear power plant north of San Francisco at Bodega Bay. He chaired the hard-fought but unsuccessful campaign for California's Nuclear Safeguards Initiative, one of the initiatives on nuclear power that went to a vote in eighteen states in 1976.

After directing the state Department of Forestry for three years as an appointee of Governor Jerry Brown, Pesonen had most recently been an eleventh-hour Brown appointee to the superior court for Contra Costa County. But after only two years, his career as a judge ended as abruptly as it began when an opposing candidate foiled his bid for reelection.

Returning to private law practice early in 1985 but unhappy in his work, Pesonen seized upon the idea of becoming general manager of the East Bay Regional Park District. He saw Kessel's invitation to apply as "wonderful."

The board, however, failed to communicate exactly what it wanted from its new administrator. "They were looking for somebody who could completely reform the organization," Pesonen recalled. There was no job description and no contract, just a broad charter to "serve at their pleasure and fix the place."

Upon assuming his new post in September 1985, General Manager Pesonen quickly set to work making changes. "I reoriented the lines of authority with a strong emphasis on natural resource protection and created a new section called land stewardship," he said. "I brought in a new person [Kevin Shea, from state government] . . . to head that up."

Pesonen also plucked from Sacramento a new deputy, Bob Connelly, who had most recently been his right hand at the Department of Forestry. Connelly would now reprise that role as the District's second-in-command, leading the team of assistant general managers and indirectly supervising the entire staff.

Administrative employees could not help but notice a change of management style. Upon arriving for work in the morning they began to find instructions Connelly had left the previous evening in their typewriters. These missives, typed in capital letters on partial sheets of paper, often ended simply enough: "DO IT NOW."

As General Manager Pesonen's assessment of the District progressed, he proceeded with little fanfare to fire several key staff members, including some who had made their careers with the District.

"In Sacramento, the governor comes in and he gets all new department heads, so [Pesonen] thought that's what he should do here with the East Bay Regional Park District," Trudeau said later.

Director Ted Radke agreed. "He ran the District like a state agency," he said.

In public affairs, Pesonen released two members of the existing staff and hired Janet Cobb—another contact from his days in Sacramento—as assistant general manager. Cobb brought high energy to the leadership of both public affairs and the Regional Parks Foundation. She soon overhauled the District's publications to achieve a more professional look.

Financial practices got a thorough shakeup under Pesonen's hand as well, including a new emphasis on funding land acquisition through borrowing—to the tune of $17 million in revenue bonds—while dipping into future funding for operations. But with limited sources, both borrowing and spending began to outweigh the agency's ability to roll with the economic punches.

In an odd twist, just as California fought its way into economic recovery, the District found itself on shaky ground. The budget reserve, tapped only sparingly since the 1940s, was now severely depleted, while funding of critical maintenance and equipment had suffered some neglect.

"That $17 million 'loan' for land acquisition was a claim against operational funds for the next twenty years," Kent said.

Pesonen's financial and management woes were compounded by the short tenure of his deputy, Connelly—who fled back to Sacramento after only a year—and by a deterioration in his own relations with the board. Although he survived an early vote of confidence on his management practices, he lost further support—and his fourth vote—after employees brought complaints, both personal and professional, against him. By early 1988, the damage was done.

"There was talk that maybe I should resign," Pesonen recalled. The board made clear it would allow him to exit quietly, and when he got a feeler about going to work at a law firm, he quickly accepted.

"I wasn't happy at the park district," he said later. "I had never been happy after about the first year."

Also, in one of the great ironies of the District's fifty-year history, Pesonen's views of environmentalism and park management had clashed with those of the very individuals who had so eagerly recruited him. Instead of being a "strict" preservationist within the regional parks, he favored providing facilities and programs that would bring people out into the wilderness, which he believed would make them better citizens.

"That's an old notion in the United States," Pesonen said. "It goes back to Jefferson."

Although board members held a range of views, Pesonen encountered in some of them a strong push for land acquisition—though not always in keeping with the master plan—and an equally strong resistance to providing picnic tables or other basic equipment for taxpaying citizens to use on that same land.

"I think there was a certain amount of racism in it, too, or cultural bias, anyway," Pesonen said. The District should be in the business of supplying access and amenities, he felt, especially at parks heavily used by low-income people and ethnic minorities who, after all, might have few nearby options for outdoor recreation.

In all, David Pesonen managed the District for only two-and-a-half years, ultimately serving as a bridge between two significant and stable periods of leadership. Though short, his term sharply altered the finances, the staff, and the stewardship of the parks themselves. He did elevate the role of planning, urging both the board and the staff to think farther ahead about land acquisition and other major projects. He ordered a comprehensive list of future projects compiled but departed before its value could be realized.

———————————

With Pesonen gone, the board once more faced the task of recruiting a general manager. Again they offered the job to Acting General Manager Kent, but again he turned it down.

## California Association of Recreation & Park Districts

Created in 1958 to improve the quality and efficiency of recreation and park districts, the California Association of Recreation & Park Districts (CARPD) is governed by a board of directors representing member districts throughout the state. In addition to tracking legislation and other issues, CARPD provides member districts with reduced rates on workers' compensation coverage and on liability and property damage insurance. Each spring, CARPD hosts an annual conference and makes awards to recognize outstanding programming, facilities, and service to the community by member districts.

The East Bay Regional Park District's general manager since 1988, Pat O'Brien, chaired the statewide efforts of CARPD's legislative committee for seven years while serving as general manager of the Southgate Recreation and Park District in Sacramento (1981–1988), also playing a key role in planning, organizing, and supporting the annual CARPD conferences. He won the CARPD President's Special Award in 2005 in recognition of his commitment to recreation and park efforts (and the overall recreation and parks movement) in California.

CARPD also named the District in the following honors:

**1996**   Outstanding Organization, Regional Parks Foundation

**2003**   Best New Facility, Camp Arroyo

**2009**   Best Marketing and Communications, Measure WW public information
Best Innovative Program (large district), Trails Challenge Program
Honorary Life Membership, Director Carol Severin of Ward 3

"I don't like what general managers do," Kent said later. "I don't like politics, and I don't like finance."

The board sought out other candidates and got some talented prospects, including the executive director of the Bay Conservation and Development Commission, a top planner from Contra Costa County, and a park professional from the East Coast. Back in 1985, Pat O'Brien had been excited by the possibility of leaving Southgate Recreation and Park District in Sacramento to take over the much larger and more challenging East Bay Regional Park District. But in 1988, after being passed over for the job and then witnessing the swift rise and fall of General Manager Pesonen, O'Brien was apprehensive.

"Oh, my God," he said to himself. "They're going to ask me again."

Over the course of seventeen years—the same length of time Trudeau had managed East Bay parks—O'Brien had risen through the ranks at Southgate, progressing from aquatics supervisor to sports and aquatics director and then to recreation superintendent within three years. As general manager since 1980, he enjoyed excellent relations with a five-member elected board.

While at Southgate, O'Brien also had amassed a depth of experience as a liaison with both the executive and legislative branches of state government. For years he chaired the legislative committees of two statewide organizations for park professionals. Never before had one person represented both simultaneously; no one since has attempted it.

The first of these, the California Association of Recreation & Park Districts, wanted a legislative representative who was located in Sacramento. Asked to serve "almost by default" owing to his proximity to the capital, O'Brien agreed.

"It was an informal but pretty powerful position," he recalled later.

Soon he was asked to become legislative chair for the California Park & Recreation Society as well, and again he accepted. He arranged for the society to contract with Bob Houston's lobbying agency—the same one used by Southgate and the East Bay parks—gaining significant political clout for the thousands of members. Working with colleagues north and south, he also helped piece together the statewide Community Parklands Act of 1986 (Proposition 43), a $100 million bond issue for acquiring, developing, and improving local and regional parks, beaches, and recreational areas.

Although his direct contact with state government was primarily legislative, O'Brien kept a close eye on the executive branch as well. When Governor Jerry Brown funded grant programs for which parks might be eligible, O'Brien worked closely with state agency staff members to secure monies for Southgate.

In the larger picture, the environmental movement was coming into its own during the seventies and early eighties and was a priority for Brown while he was governor for two terms starting in 1975. In addition to naming David Pesonen as forestry director, Brown had appointed to his administration such cutting-edge thinkers as Sim Van der Ryn, a leader of the sustainable architecture movement, as state architect and publisher Stewart Brand as special adviser. He selected John Bryson—who would later become CEO of Southern California Edison and help found the Natural Resources Defense Council—to chair the state water board.

## California Park & Recreation Society
## and the East Bay Regional Park District

The California Park & Recreation Society (CPRS) is a nonprofit professional organization providing public advocacy, career development, networking, and resources for the park and recreation field in California. Founded in 1946, CPRS has thousands of individual members as well as 175 agency members.

The East Bay Regional Park District's general manager since 1988, Pat O'Brien, for seven years chaired the statewide efforts of the CPRS legislative committee while serving as general manager of the Southgate Recreation and Park District in Sacramento (1981–1988) during the critical period after the statewide property tax revolt, Proposition 13, passed in June 1978. O'Brien was selected as CPRS's Outstanding Legislative Leader for 1983 and its Outstanding Professional for 1988. During that period he played a key advocacy role in the successful passage of statewide park bond measures, notably Proposition 43 in 1986 and Proposition 70 in 1988.

He also won the CPRS president's award for 1988 and the Professional Hall of Fame Award for 2002. In recognition of his continuing influence on legislative matters for the park and recreation field, CPRS in 1988 renamed its legislative award the Pat O'Brien Legislative Award.

Rosemary Cameron, assistant general manager of public affairs, also served as a legislative liaison for the District and co-chaired the CPRS annual legislative conference. She was awarded the CPRS Professional of the Year award in 1986 in recognition of her efforts on behalf of the statewide legislative program.

But neither the public nor the media was quite ready for the young Governor Brown, who was, in O'Brien's words, "a hop, skip, and a jump ahead of the environmental movement itself, in all kinds of ways."

In 1978, the forward-thinking Brown proposed a satellite for emergency communications. The idea was so startlingly new that columnist Mike Royko dubbed Brown "Governor Moonbeam," a nickname that stuck long after many citizens could recall what prompted it. Brown suffered for his advanced notions about the environment and technology, but many ideas he championed then have since become realities that Americans take for granted every day.

Throughout this period, some traditional park and recreation leaders may have felt chilled by the strong wind of environmentalism that was now vying with them for public support and state funding. Individual environmentalists liked and supported parks, to be sure, but as a group they were not seen as particularly friendly toward parks. Their focus was on preserving land, not using it.

As legislative discussions began to display a conflict of views on public access—the same conflict playing out at the District—the legislature itself suffered some confusion. The environmental movement's lobbying arm, the Planning and Conservation League, might now, for example, pass legislation out of committee that encompassed parks, which were accustomed to tending their own interests in Sacramento. Similarly, a park bond measure might include environmental provisions that were not necessarily related to parks. Even when the goals of various interest groups were the same, their methods and priorities sometimes differed dramatically.

———————————

By 1988, for the second time in three years, the East Bay Regional Park District needed a new leader. Sure enough, Dick Trudeau urged Pat O'Brien to apply a second time for the position of general manager, cajoling him daily with phone calls. Director John O'Donnell approached him too, even bringing two new board colleagues, Kathryn Petersen and Jocelyn Combs, up to Sacramento to meet him.

Seymour Greben, a Los Angeles park administrator and longtime consultant to the District, advised O'Brien not to apply again. "Don't even think about it," he said. "The board has bad attitudes, and they are unhappy. They can't get along with each other."

But in spite of his own misgivings and those of others, O'Brien found himself irresistibly drawn to the idea that, with the right leadership, the board could become more effective in its work. David Pesonen was exceedingly bright, but maybe he had not known how to work constructively with an elective board. Was it possible he simply did not have the street smarts to excel in this setting?

O'Brien himself had an instinct for working with board members, both individually and as a group. He had done it successfully for eight years as general manager at Southgate and, as a matter of fact, rather liked it. But there was no escaping the differences between the two systems. The East Bay Regional Park District had seven directors, not five. And while they were dedicated, active, and knowledgeable about parks, their process for working together had veered sharply off course. That, in turn, had paralyzed communication and compromised procedures used by the staff. The system itself was fragmented and would have to be repaired.

"I know how to figure that out," O'Brien told himself. "I can do that."

By the time O'Brien applied, on the last possible day, O'Donnell had brought his influence to bear on the board. Mary Jefferds had assumed the rotating presidency, and during a Saturday interview at the Skyline Boulevard headquarters in Oakland, O'Brien was taken aback when she began talking salary.

Standing in the foyer with Donn Black, the District's in-house attorney, during a break, O'Brien tried to make sense of the interview.

"They've already figured out they want to hire you," Black said.

The interview had become a negotiation. Taking the situation in stride, O'Brien surprised the seven directors by insisting upon a multiyear contract where none had existed before. "If an eighteen-year-old baseball player gets a contract, so do I," he told them.

Lawyers for both sides swarmed over the details and the hours ticked by, but together the board and their new general manager struck a deal that very day. O'Brien would administer the East Bay Regional Park District for an initial contract period of four years.

Along with impeccable credentials and strong ties to the legislative process in Sacramento, O'Brien would now bring to the District a quiet demeanor and self-effacing humor that masked the wily mentality of a boxer. His actual boxing career had spanned only a few years in high school, but his fascination with strategy had taken root then and grown steadily over the years. While pursuing both a bachelor's and a master's degree in philosophy, and through three years on the East Coast in the U.S. Army Security Agency, he had observed the behavior of others and learned how to tailor actions to circumstances in order to win. With seventeen years at Southgate under his belt, his power of strategic thinking had been highly refined.

Although nobody at the District knew it yet, Pat O'Brien was at heart a boxer still, fiercely competitive and tactically adroit. His mental acuity and economy of movement would prove essential for the controversies that lay ahead.

Morgan Territory Regional Preserve, acquired in 1975, increased by 643 acres in 1988 and, with subsequent additions, stands at 4,860 acres today. Its grassy sandstone hills and lowland valleys are home to a rich variety of flora and fauna, including this stately old oak.

# In Memoriam: Richard C. Trudeau (1920–2004)

Three general managers of the East Bay Regional Park District at Trudeau's retirement party in 1985: Pat O'Brien (general manager since 1988), William Penn Mott Jr. (1962–1967), and Richard C. Trudeau (1968–1985)

For more than forty years, Richard "Dick" C. Trudeau exerted a profound influence on the leadership and growth of the East Bay Regional Park District and on the parks and recreation field. Hired by William Penn Mott Jr. in 1963 to develop public relations for the District, he played a key role in the successful annexation of Contra Costa County in 1964.

Succeeding Mott as general manager, Trudeau led the agency for seventeen years (1968–1985), working with the board to carry out an unparalleled program of expansion. Together they brought 40,000 acres under the agency's protection at such sites as Briones Regional Park, Las Trampas Regional Wilderness, and Point Pinole and Martinez regional shorelines. With his land chief, Hulet Hornbeck, Trudeau also overcame initial public doubt to establish the Lafayette-Moraga Regional Trail, one of the first multiuse urban trails in the nation. "It was really a pioneer thing to put in urban trails at that time," said General Manager Pat O'Brien.

Even after Proposition 13, the property tax revolt of 1978, devastated the financing structure of local governments, Trudeau stayed the course through a series of innovative steps for alternative financing of both land acquisition and park operations. He established the Regional Parks Foundation to raise private funds, also winning millions of state and federal dollars through avenues that had never before been tried.

General Manager Dick Trudeau (on right) with Ed Meese, counsel to President Ronald Reagan, at the dedication of San Leandro Bay Regional Shoreline (later renamed to honor Dr. Martin Luther King Jr.) in 1979

"The entire face of parks and recreation was to change dramatically," recalled Chris Jarvi, Trudeau's longtime Southern California colleague, "and Dick Trudeau was to rise as one of the most important influences of that time." Upon seeing Trudeau in action for the first time during that post–Proposition 13 period, Jarvi came away with the impression of someone floating across the room as he moved, not merely walking. "I distinctly remember thinking that this man exuded an energy I had rarely seen in my lifetime," Jarvi said.

In bringing that energy to bear on East Bay parks—the pounding of his typewriter audible downstairs in the land department of the Skyline headquarters as he masterminded a state park bond or corporate sponsorship late into the night—Trudeau also earned the recognition of his peers, winning the National Recreation and Park Association's award of professional excellence in 1970.

Trudeau initiated the District's first professional master plan, resulting in the 1973 document that has remained in use, with periodic revisions, ever since. He was the first to hire an independent attorney for the District to replace the county counsel, and he established a lobbying presence in Sacramento and in Washington, D.C. He emphasized the highest standards for public safety, including significant regional planning for wildfire prevention and response.

After retiring in 1985, Trudeau continued to volunteer his time in pursuit of parks. He helped to pass the District's local capital-funding initiatives, starting with Measure AA in 1988, as well as multiple state park bonds. He founded the nonprofit California Greenways to support regional trails and greenways, and he served as executive director of the Mott Foundation. Trudeau earned further recognition in retirement, including the park profession's prestigious Pugsley Award in 1990, the California Park & Recreation Society's fellowship award and a National Park Service president's award, both in 1991, and a national conservation award from Chevron Corporation in 1992. He continued his proactive approach to life and work, taking on Bill Mott's ringing challenge anew each day: "Vision is a powerful thing," Mott said, "a dream based on a clear perception of the future, combined with a commitment to take the necessary steps to make it happen."

Photographer and environmental activist Bob Walker, who served on the Measure AA campaign committee, embarked on a personal crusade to talk directly with as many voters as possible in the months leading up to the November 1988 election. The slide show of his photographs became a hallmark of the campaign and included many stunning images, such as this one of an oak tree arcing over the green hills of Pleasanton Ridge.

## Chapter 5

# Voters

*People get nervous when environmentalists and developers sit down and negotiate an agreement. A good environmentalist is not supposed to compromise, and developers are not supposed to give environmentalists political leverage.*

—MARK EVANOFF, People for Open Space, 1988

Taking the helm of the East Bay Regional Park District on an acting basis after General Manager David Pesonen's departure on April 1, 1988, Jerry Kent soon got a pleasant jolt from the outside world. In the big financial picture, the District relied heavily on its base of property tax revenue to fund operations and to acquire land for parks. Recently, however, the agency had taken a $17 million loan to buy land, increasing debt without spreading the burden over a variety of sources. In the post–Proposition 13 era of reduced property taxes, that approach could succeed only so long.

Lately, though, Californians had shown strong support for protecting natural areas and enlarging park systems. As recently as 1986 they had passed a $100 million statewide park bond, the Community Parklands Act (Proposition 43). In Sacramento, Pat O'Brien had collaborated with the chief of staff to Senator Robert Presley, the act's sponsor, on a per capita distribution formula. For the first time all eligible park agencies, no matter how small, would win funds.

Dick Trudeau, the District's former general manager, cochaired that 1986 campaign in the early months of his retirement, drawing upon his vast list of contacts and working long days right up until the June election. Some 67 percent of voters gave the nod, an outcome so good that park advocates might easily have rested their case. But after that victory, neither they nor the voters were in a mood to slow down.

Now, with the District's administrative leadership in transition and the economy showing signs of recovery, another statewide park bond would appear on the ballot in June 1988. Brought forth by the Planning and Conservation League, Proposition 70 would go to voters as a citizen initiative rather than a legislative one. The 1986 measure, at $100 million, had seemed substantial at the time, but Proposition 70 would propose a bond issue of a cool $776 million.

Again, California voters came through. At 65 percent in favor, their level of support stood nearly as high as before. Under the Public Resources Code, local entities—including special districts—could apply for funds.

The board of directors absorbed this happy news and wasted no time acting upon it. The District had received more than $2 million in bond funding from the 1986 act; now it could pursue eligible projects on a grander scale.

Meanwhile, Kent worked to keep the District operating smoothly in the wake of Pesonen's hasty departure. While the board sought a permanent general manager, he responded to every imaginable issue brought forth by members of an anxious staff at headquarters and in the field. As weeks turned to months, Kent's steady presence worked its magic, just as it had for the past twenty-five years.

Assistant General Manager Jerry Kent (at podium) congratulates staff honorees at an Operations Department awards ceremony.

Gentle, unflappable, and given to diplomacy in all things, Kent had attended Oregon State University for three years before returning to his native California to complete a degree in park management at California State University, Sacramento. Hired at the District as a "park groundsman" in 1962, he was promoted to supervisor of Tilden Park the following year and went on to a variety of managerial roles before becoming second-in-command during much of Trudeau's tenure as general manager.

For many years Kent had set the style of the District's internal organization. While Trudeau worked closely with the board and served as liaison with the outside world, pursuing complicated land deals and cultivating the legislature, Kent operated the parks and implemented Trudeau's and the board's goals. He knew every park, every staff member, and practically every shovel, truck, and fire hose, too. Having held almost every job in the field and in the office, he was not easily surprised.

But in early June 1988, when Director Jocelyn Combs visited Jerry Kent one morning with a bold new idea about finance, he was not quite prepared. In a one-two punch, Combs introduced the matter she had been working on with Director Ted Radke. That afternoon Janet Cobb, assistant general manager of public affairs, expanded on it, with Mark Evanoff of People for Open Space at her side.

In Contra Costa County, they noted, open space advocates and some cities had worked to defeat a 1986 transportation bond that carried a half-cent increase in the sales tax. The suggestion being floated now—to pursue a larger strategy for growth management by revising the transportation bond and including open space provisions for regional parks—might invite a second failure, especially if business and environmental interests did not buy in at an early stage.

In Alameda County, voters already had passed a 1986 transportation bond that made no open space provisions for land or trails. It made no sense to combine transportation with parks there. But in keeping with the master-plan priority to acquire parklands using funds from new sources, the District should go to voters again, perhaps with a separate two-county measure for parks alone.

Kent saw the attraction of this idea, but he knew only too well the complexity of the big picture. A local park bond measure would require a two-thirds majority to pass, rather than the simple majority of a statewide bond. Although both counties had begun to think regionally about land use, they had starkly different needs, priorities, and players. Agricultural and ranching interests, not to mention environmental groups and developers, would bring multiple issues to the table. With the November election just five months away, how could a workable plan for a separate park bond be realized?

Kent dug deep into his well of knowledge and experience. In truth, he had to agree that the District stood a much better chance of success by going it alone, separate from transportation, especially if the business community and open space advocates pledged to participate in the planning and not oppose the measure. Both he and the board understood the critical need for some $200 million from new sources to acquire land. If they hoped to achieve any growth whatsoever, the funds would have to come from somewhere. The recent pattern of spending reserves for that purpose—or borrowing without a clear way to repay loans—could not be sustained.

———————————

As an exploratory step, the board scheduled a special "information only" public meeting for June 14, 1988, to introduce the proposed park bond measure as an outgrowth of Contra Costa's transportation measure. The latter measure, they explained, with its half-cent increase in the sales tax, was being reworked for a second try through the Transportation Partnership Commission set up by county supervisors and the confer-

## Park Advisory Committee

The Park Advisory Committee (PAC) had its roots in the early 1970s when the East Bay Regional Park District formed two large public advisory bodies to aid its master planning process. One outgrowth of that master plan of 1973 was the consolidation of those two committees into a single permanent advisory body, which has continued and built upon its role as an important liaison with the community. By seeking the PAC's input at an early stage of planning and setting policy, the board could give further voice to its constituents.

In the 1990s, the PAC diversified and revitalized its membership by instituting a maximum of two consecutive four-year terms for members, who are selected by the District's board of directors from their own nominations and those of local government entities in both Alameda and Contra Costa counties. The PAC establishes specific goals each year, as well as pursuing a list of ongoing general goals. It makes recommendations to the board of directors on a great variety of projects for park and trail acquisition and stewardship, providing a critical liaison with the citizens the District exists to serve. Some PAC members also serve as ongoing volunteer ambassadors, representing the District's interests to the public.

ence of mayors. The now-separate park bond would be financed through modest property tax assessments in both counties.

Furthermore, the two measures together, transportation and parks, represented significant growth management and open space protection for years to come. With some 6,000 new homes proposed for development on the ridgelands of both counties, and with waste disposal needs already escalating into "the dump wars," thoughtful planning for the region's future would be essential.

The June 14 public meeting also recapped the previous week's election results. Voters in both counties had just passed the statewide park bond measure, Proposition 70—and also the similar Proposition 43 in 1986—at higher rates than voters elsewhere in California. That evidence supported the case for putting a park measure forth soon. Proposition 70 funds, though significant, would support only a handful of District parks.

With public consultation under way, the board members looked ahead to June 21. In only a week they would decide one of the most critical matters in the District's fifty-four-year history. If they approved a park bond measure in principle, the next few months would test the mettle of every one of them and would place an almost inconceivable burden on the shoulders of Kent and his staff. If they voted down the proposal, the District's financial future and capacity for growth, along with the future of the region's open space, would remain in serious doubt.

Kent's reluctance about the bond had given way to tentative support, but the board had split. Directors Radke and Combs favored the idea, but Mary Jefferds and Kathryn Petersen stood firmly opposed to the concept and the financial risks. Harlan Kessel, John O'Donnell, and Jim Duncan occupied the middle ground, tending toward cautious support.

Radke had advised on Contra Costa's 1986 transportation measure and felt that the county should try again on transportation while also supporting a separate park bond. Early on, he had consulted Hulet Hornbeck, the District's former land chief, whose vast knowledge of Contra Costa matched his own.

"Hulet was all for it," Radke said.

With positions thus staked out, Radke knew beforehand that a family camping trip would cause him to miss the momentous meeting. He drove to the Plumas National Forest, where he tried to put the bond measure out of his mind. But it kept nagging, so he hiked out to a pay phone and called Janet Cobb. She told him trouble was afoot with Directors Jefferds, Kessel, and Petersen.

"They might not come to the meeting," Cobb told him.

**"Keep Them Here Forever...
For Only Forty-Seven Cents a Month."**

## VOTE
# YES on Measure 'AA'

This 1988 campaign brochure emphasized the low cost of preserving wildlife and open space through creation of regional parks.

Each had offered a reason for a possible absence. But as all seven directors knew, the bond proposal would need five votes, a two-thirds majority, rather than the usual four to pass. With time so short, they must approve it immediately, also authorizing the necessary steps to place it on the ballot. Without a vote, the whole thing would collapse.

Radke packed up his gear and sped back to Oakland, a drive of six hours, meeting his colleagues in the borrowed boardroom of the Bay Area Rapid Transit (BART) agency's Oakland headquarters. Jefferds and Kessel had appeared after all, along with Combs, O'Donnell, and Duncan. Only Petersen was absent.

As board president, Jefferds called them to order, knowing the time to equivocate had run out. She, for one, thought the proposed bond amount, estimated at $200 million or more, was too much and had no intention of supporting it. Thus began an excruciating debate. The crush of recent events—combined with a meeting process none too faithful to Robert's *Rules of Order*—now brought tensions to the fore. As afternoon turned to evening, the hopes of agreement faded, revived, and faded again.

But when at last Jefferds put the matter to a vote, the result was, miraculously, unanimous. The "ayes" had it. Jefferds's own position had shifted, and all six had voted to leap together into an unprecedented venture that would make or break everything for the next twenty years.

If they hoped to meet the election department deadline, they must adopt a formal resolution by August 2, only six weeks hence. Before adjourning, they called for a poll of voters and broad input from local governments. They named a financial adviser and bond counsel, then approved pages of board and staff assignments before dispersing to begin their own work.

The board's legislative committee—Radke, Combs, and Kessel—would lead the push for public approval of the bond measure. They would shepherd the effort through four-and-a-half grueling months until the November 8 election, working closely with Kent and his staff, especially Cobb and the in-house attorney, Ellen Maldonado, on bond details and the ballot-measure text.

A volunteer campaign committee was formed to include Cobb, who would participate on her own time, former District managers Dick Trudeau and Hulet Hornbeck, former controller Ed Loss, Concord mayor Byron Campbell, Mark Evanoff, and Bob Walker, the extraordinary activist and photographer whose images would bring the campaign alive.

Both the board and volunteer committees moved out into the trenches to head off organized opposition and cement the unlikely alliance of environmentalists and land developers.

In an unusual development, Cobb declared that she would make a substantial personal loan to the campaign so it could begin immediately the gritty work of getting the word out to voters. She wrote a check for $15,000 in "seed money," and the campaign committee set to work compiling maps, photos, brochures, and a slide show to ready themselves for a blitz of publicity with voters, legislators, newspapers, advocacy groups, and local governments.

Contracting with behavioral scientist George Manross of the Strategy Research Institute, the District began assessing voter support, while Kent, Cobb, and Evanoff talked with city representatives to assure them that the proposed park bond would address their main concern, revenue sharing. On his own, Evanoff had written to cities in mid-May to float the bond idea. Although responding favorably, several city representatives insisted that they could accept only a fifty-fifty split of funds with the District. The rancorous history of dividing up funds from state park bonds stretched back two decades, so resolving that element would be critical to winning city support.

As the campaign progressed, every city council, service club, and advocacy organization got a personal visit and detailed presentation. Some board members were out every night of the week carrying to elected officials and ordinary citizens a message of great returns on small investments, to be made through a slight increase in property taxes: "For 47 cents a month—less than the price of a cup of coffee—each of you can do unbelievable good for our system of regional parks."

As for exactly what good that might be, the land division was racing to refine a list of land acquisition projects to include in the bond measure. Bob Doyle, who had succeeded Hornbeck as land chief, worked closely with Kent and other key staff members, especially planning chief Tom Mikkelsen and financial whiz Dave Collins, to rank and establish dollar figures for acquiring and developing new parks, enlarging existing ones, building trails, and protecting creeks. Forced to hold planning sessions on the fly, they made notes and diagrams on any paper surface they could find.

"Jerry Kent used napkins," Doyle said later. "I used maps."

In a matter of days they had to nail down a design for land acquisition and associated costs that would guide them for the next twenty years. Their work had to be fast and it had to be good. As the maps proliferated and the evaluation of land parcels continued, they dissected every acre they hoped to add. They analyzed each surrounding acre as well, knowing they would have to make their case in the court of public opinion.

"We could bring in the concept of defensible boundaries," Doyle said.

Doyle and his team revised the projected acreage upward and then upward again. At last they settled upon ambitious figures they knew they could uphold. If the bond measure passed they would pledge to create 7,500 acres of new parks while enlarging existing parks by 20,000 acres.

Meeting on July 5, 1988, the board reviewed a preliminary public-opinion survey, which confirmed the District's high level of credibility with constituents and indicated that a two-thirds majority could be achieved. More poll results would come within weeks. They also approved Cobb's proposal to conduct focus groups, and they debated the amount and term of the bond.

Next, the directors again considered options for sharing revenue with local entities. Kent had appointed an advisory committee from among city park and recreation agencies, but no clear recommendation had yet emerged. Should 80 percent go to the District and 20 percent to cities, or would a 60-40 split be acceptable, as the District's bond counsel recommended? Several directors said their constituents wanted a 50-50 split.

July 19, another regularly scheduled board day, dawned scorchingly hot in the East Bay. The Democratic National Convention had just hit full swing in Atlanta, reinvigorating the promise of a good voter turnout in a presidential election year. Although the board had voted a month ago to proceed, the bond amount and the split of funds with park and recreation agencies had yet to be decided. Without consensus on these crucial elements, they knew, the whole plan might falter.

Sweating profusely in the extreme heat of that early afternoon, Jerry Kent entered BART headquarters and hurried to the boardroom to take his accustomed place alongside other managers, staff, and consultants, twenty in all. George Manross and his associate, Ana Maria del Rio, presented the board with detailed poll results. Seventy-one percent of voters favored a sizable bond for East Bay parks. Citizens had passed statewide Proposition 70 because they were confident that tangible projects were associated with specific costs. A similarly clear plan to offer concrete benefits in regional parks was something local voters would understand and support.

The dollar amount of the bond also had been subjected to rigorous study. The pollsters now recommended $225 million, taking into account voters' general support but also their threshold for increased property taxes, which would not exceed $10 annually per $100,000 of assessed property value.

The matter of revenue sharing with cities was not so easily settled. City recreation and park agencies were still gunning for a substantial share, yet poll results showed faint public enthusiasm for funding them. Voters did, however, indicate a willingness to support the Oakland Zoo. In the heat of that late afternoon, cooled only by pitchers of ice water, the board debated the revenue-sharing possibilities. Finally, Director Combs urged serious consideration of a new formula, easy to remember yet heavily weighted toward the District, which was, after all, the measure's sponsor. One by one the other directors agreed until Combs won unanimous support. Together they would present to the outside world a united front and a decision rendered.

The ballot language would specify 75 percent of the $225 million bond for the District and 25 percent for distribution to city and other local park entities. Extending the same formula to the District's own $168 million share of the total, 75 percent of that amount would go to land acquisition and 25 percent to development of park facilities.

The Park Advisory Committee addressed the board to report a split vote, 11–11, on supporting the measure, owing to the whole concept of sharing funds, in any amount, with cities. Nevertheless, the board unanimously pronounced the bond measure a "go," adopting a resolution to place it on the November ballot before the confidence of voters slipped away in some future economic slump.

As president, Jefferds immediately wrote to mayors and agency heads in both counties to announce the forthcoming measure and the revenue-sharing provision. Some cities never came to support the 75 and 25 percent formula. But even officials who had pressed for a 50-50 split, such as those in Pleasanton and at the Hayward Area Recreation and Park District, could agree that the share to be distributed locally, more than $56 million, was no small change.

On August 2, Kent and his staff carried to BART headquarters the materials for a formal resolution by the board. As president, Jefferds had now fully embraced the bond. In a show of solidarity that would have been unthinkable only weeks before, she and her six colleagues moved, seconded, and unanimously adopted the Regional Open Space, Wildlife, Shoreline, and Parks Bond for the counties of Alameda and Contra Costa.

As the extraordinary efforts of the board and staff continued, enthusiasm for the measure appeared to build, shaping an unlikely alliance of interest groups. Cities

Jerry D. Kent retired in 2003 as assistant general manager for operations, leading the largest district division for much of his exemplary 41-year career. In 1988, he was serving as acting general manager when Measure AA was conceived, formulated, and approved by voters.

supported it, the business community was behind it, and open space advocates were actively promoting it. Even the District's own union—reluctant to support ambitious land acquisition with no new money for park operations—came to agree, under Jack Kenny's leadership, that tax revenue from regional growth would boost the general fund enough to cover staff increases in new and expanding parks.

While formal presentations and meetings by the board and the volunteer campaign committee continued, other gatherings of interested parties unfolded as well. The world-champion rodeo cowboy and steer wrestler Jack Roddy hosted a dinner at his 2,000-acre ranch south of Antioch. Prominent ranchers aired their concerns about growth, land use, and the perceived encroachment of parks on their territory. Before the night was over, Roddy's advocacy for both ballot measures, parks and transportation, had convinced his peers. Now they pledged to help spread the good word.

"I'm not bragging," Roddy has said since, "but the long and the short of it is I've never lost a fight because I don't lie. And when I do get into something, I know the subject."

As the summer wore on, Janet Cobb surprised Kent and the board by announcing her intention to take a leave of absence from public affairs in order to work on the campaign. Having seeded the effort early on with a loan of personal funds, she now made an even more astonishing move. Taking out a second mortgage on her home, she made another personal loan to the campaign, this time in the amount of $30,000. As always, she was thinking big and moving fast in order to succeed. Nobody at the District had ever seen anything like it.

When at last the election department released absentee ballots in late September and Kent got his first look, he was aghast. The park bond was but one in a long list of measures voters were being asked to decide. Statewide, nine other bond initiatives also sought funding from taxpayers, alongside twenty additional nonfinancial items. Myriad local measures had qualified as well. Voters in both counties would face the longest ballots in their history. Having run out of single letters, the registrar had dubbed the park bond "Measure AA," and its position on the ballot was dead last. Would voters find the measure on the last page of their ballots, much less pass it?

On election day, November 8, Measure AA campaign leaders pushed themselves to the brink to help get out the vote and then withdrew, exhausted, to watch the returns on television. The answer they sought, however, was nowhere to be found. Early returns on Measure AA were too close to call, the middle returns closer still. By the wee hours they dared to hope both the park bond and the Contra Costa transportation measure, Measure C, had prevailed, but neither race had yet been called.

The next day's early morning news produced no clear result either. The counting of absentee ballots continued, passing the transportation measure but yielding no final result for the park bond.

After ten days a decision came down. Measure AA had won 68 percent of the vote over both counties, exceeding the two-thirds majority requirement by less than two percentage points. In Contra Costa the measure had fallen slightly short, but Alameda County had put it over the top. The East Bay Regional Park District had survived a period of turmoil and risen to fight again. Now it had a future.

Jerry Kent gathered key staff members and congratulated them: Tom Mikkelsen, Mike Anderson, Dave Collins, Bob Doyle, and, of course, Janet Cobb. This success belonged to everyone, Kent told them, not only managers, but each member of the board, the administrative staff, and the field staff.

Janet Cobb, assistant general manager, Public Affairs (center), with staff members who worked on the public information program for Measure AA

With the bond providing a new mechanism to fund land acquisition, never again would the District teeter so hazardously on the edge of financial collapse. Together the board and staff had met every possible challenge of a large, complex public agency. Now, with a new leader on deck and a financial future too, the only thing ahead was a lot of hard work. Compared to what they had just been through, Kent thought, that would be a snap.

Beautiful Lake Chabot is a 315-acre reservoir built in 1874–1875 as a primary source of water for the East Bay. Leased from the East Bay Municipal Utility District, Lake Chabot Regional Park is now popular for fishing, boating, hiking, biking, and picnicking.

## Chapter 6

# Transition

*A board member's role and responsibilities include making and approving appropriate district policy, community leadership, strategic thinking, and developing a board's vision.*

—"How to Be an Effective Board Member" workshop,
California Special Districts Association, 2008

From his first day as general manager of the East Bay Regional Park District, Pat O'Brien brought a calm and measured presence to a highly charged environment. As it happened, his arrival in November 1988 coincided with the pleasant but urgent task of managing $225 million in new bond funding from Measure AA, approved by voters just days before.

In spite of the challenges ahead, O'Brien could scarcely contain his enthusiasm. He had seen just about everything by managing the Southgate Recreation and Park District in Sacramento for eight years—and working there for a total of seventeen years—but the East Bay agency offered a unique interface between cities and undeveloped areas. The geography featured every imaginable landscape, from remote high peaks to bayside wetlands. As the largest regional park district of its kind in the nation, it had a history of setting more trends than it followed.

"Certainly, you could have an open space agency in an open space rural area, which would be wonderful and very interesting, I'm sure," O'Brien said later. "But here you have the collision of ultimate urban issues with open space protection and wildlife habitat. There's such a diversity of properties here. It's a dream for the person who loves parks."

Applying an entrepreneurial streak learned in the trenches at Southgate, O'Brien arranged the initial sale of the Measure AA bond issue with an eye to bringing in grants and matching funds from other sources. In addition to increasing the pace of land acquisition, the District would establish a delivery system to get AA funds committed quickly to specific land purchases.

The bond measure also included a revenue-sharing component. The District would grant 25 percent of bond funds to local park agencies in the two counties on a per capita basis. To initiate and manage this $28 million endeavor, O'Brien would need expert help, especially as potential recipients already appeared to distrust the equity of the process. After hiring the newly retired state parks grant administrator as a consultant, O'Brien called a meeting of local park and recreation directors at the Brazil Room in Tilden Park.

"I brought out Russ Porter, whom they all knew, and said he was in charge of developing this program," O'Brien recalled. "The whole place just calmed down. It was like pouring molasses over something. He had credibility with our local agency representatives, but most importantly, he had their trust."

Porter's ties to Sacramento brought some grousing from the District's own staff. But Porter was "the perfect choice" in O'Brien's view, accustomed to managing similar programs on a much larger scale. In about six months Porter had the program in place.

The bond measure took priority in those early months, but O'Brien had a few other things on his plate as well.

In getting to know others on the District's loyal and talented staff, which included many who had served the agency their whole careers, O'Brien soon saw that the physical spread of both parks and office space kept them apart from one another in important ways. Abrupt changes during David Pesonen's short tenure had left them a little suspicious about what a new general manager might do, though Acting General Manager Jerry Kent had restored trust the last few months, leading the District through the challenge of preparing the bond measure on a tight schedule.

O'Brien placed a high priority on fostering greater collaboration by the executive management team, which included the department heads of operations and interpretation (Jerry Kent), planning, design, and stewardship (Tom Mikkelsen), land acquisition (Bob Doyle), public safety (Pete Sarna), management services (Bob Owen), and public affairs (Janet Cobb)—each holding the title of assistant general manager. He analyzed the group's process for working together and identified formal changes that would improve outcomes.

The presence of an employee union added yet another dimension, one of the few aspects of management new to O'Brien. Until he could assess all personnel and salaries as a portion of the overall budget, he would create no new staff positions.

High on O'Brien's list were the seven individuals who made up the elected board of directors and to whom he would now report. Though he was well acquainted with a few of them—mainly Mary Lee Jefferds and John O'Donnell—they were, as a group, reputedly often at odds with one another. More than one previous general manager had been confounded by the details of working with them, even when aiming toward common goals.

O'Brien considered the delicate task of facilitating the board's group process and overall effectiveness. Hired with unanimous support of all seven directors, he knew from talking with one predecessor, Dick Trudeau, that it would take time to build effective working relationships with them. To that end, his game plan was simple. He would strive to find common ground, working out divisive issues and even smaller concerns at an early stage rather than battling to achieve a bare majority in the boardroom.

The East Bay Regional Park District's general manager, Pat O'Brien (far left) with the board of directors: From left are Harlan Kessel, Ted Radke, Jocelyn Combs, Jim Duncan, Carroll Williams, Oliver Holmes, and John O'Donnell.

"I remember Dick Trudeau giving me a piece of advice," O'Brien recalled. "He said, 'There are seven board members, and you've always got to get four of those.' I looked at him. 'Dick, my job is to get seven votes, not four.' "

Just as reputation and Trudeau's words implied, O'Brien found himself interacting with a board that had grown accustomed to making decisions by colliding with one another from opposing sides rather than building consensus. Some of them also directed the staff's work at times, blurring the lines between a legitimate policy-and-oversight role and a less appropriate entanglement in day-to-day management. After Trudeau's retirement in 1985, their decisions in both arenas had nearly brought the District to its knees. Now there was some rebuilding to do.

Reviewing the board's membership over the years, O'Brien identified some pivotal points in its fascinating history. One such point centered on the current president, Mary Jefferds, who exemplified a brand of citizen activism centered in powerful environmental organizations. Raised in Berkeley, Jefferds had grown up hiking and riding on protected watershed land and had developed a lifelong passion for the outdoors.

"In the early 1930s she used to rent a horse called Snowball for seventy-five cents per hour ... and ride up the trails ... into what was to become Tilden Park," said Es Anderson of the Tilden-Wildcat Horsemen's Association.

Jefferds's twenty-year environmental education career with the Audubon Society had provided ample opportunity to advocate for environmental causes and to share her knowledge with others, especially young people. She also held strong credentials in such organizations as Save the Bay, the Sierra Club, and People for Open Space.

After attending the first meeting of the Political Action Coalition for the Environment in 1970, Jefferds had helped this new "nonpartisan pressure group" in its mission to elect environmentally oriented candidates to the boards of four East Bay "special districts" sanctioned by the State of California: rapid transit (BART), bus service (AC Transit), water (East Bay Municipal Utility District, on whose master plan committee Jefferds had served), and parks (East Bay Regional Park District). When no candidate turned up for parks in 1972, she agreed to stand for election herself.

After operating since its inception in 1934 with board members who resided in and represented geographic "wards" but who were elected at large by all voters, the District had only recently, in 1967, been directed by the legislature to make a change.

"The legislators . . . said, 'Why should [the East Bay Regional Park District] be electing at large when nobody else is?'" Trudeau recalled.

"The union and a lot of other people wanted an opportunity to run candidates," he added. "You could never defeat anybody on the board [under the old system] because they were getting votes from . . . the whole district."

Then-general manager William Penn Mott Jr., with unanimous agreement of the board, would have liked to retain the at-large system. But Trudeau, sent by Mott to Sacramento to speak against pending legislation that would require voting by wards, saw instantly that he was taking up the cause too late. Making his case in a committee hearing, he noticed the legislators talking among themselves instead of listening.

"The speaker already had the votes, so I knew it was over," he said. "They weren't paying any attention."

Trudeau vowed that he would never again address legislators without first laying the groundwork with individual members before they had committed their votes. From now on he would have meaningful discussions with them early in the process, and he would have better arguments prepared.

He promised himself, too, that if he became general manager the District would hire a lobbyist to represent its interests in Sacramento. This trip to the Capitol might be an immediate loss, but the loss came with an important and lasting lesson about how to win.

"That is how I got so much of the legislation through [later]," Trudeau said. "I only lost a couple . . . [but] I usually won those back . . . the second time around."

For the moment, though, the District would begin to elect directors by ward. Like other local government entities, it would realign the wards by population after each decennial census. It was a whole new game.

———————————

Trudeau did succeed Mott as general manager in 1968, inheriting the business-oriented and stable board that had spanned Mott's five-year tenure with only a couple of seamless changes in its membership. Sure enough, the new ward system changed all that, starting in Ward 5—Hayward, Newark, Dublin, and Pleasanton—where ornithology professor Howard Cogswell drew on his environmental knowledge to unseat horticultural retailer George Roeding in 1970. The next contest, in the northwestern Ward 1, ushered in an era of real change in the board's membership.

With thirty-five miles of shoreline in both counties and encompassing the cities of Richmond, El Cerrito, Albany, Berkeley, and Emeryville, Ward 1 had an educated and left-leaning constituency that identified strongly with the new civic emphasis on the environment and the bay shoreline. The incumbent, Paul Harberts, owned a sporting goods store in Berkeley and had been active in the chamber of commerce and other business and philanthropic efforts since the 1940s. In 1968 he was approached about interviewing for a vacancy that the board would fill by appointment between elections.

"Everybody knew I had no connection whatsoever nor visible interest in parks," Harberts recalled. "But they interviewed me and subsequently appointed me."

Standing for election later that year, Harberts was the first to retain an appointed seat under the new ward election system. But four years later, in the changing world of the early 1970s, he was no match for the likes of challenger Jefferds, who ran with support from the Political Action Coalition for the Environment, the employee union, and every prominent environmental group.

"I won, which was a great shock to everybody," Jefferds said.

Not only had an incumbent lost his seat, he had lost it to a woman. As was true of many governing boards at that time, the District's leadership stretching back to the mid-1940s included only men. Although a woman had been among the first five board members in 1934—Dr. Aurelia Henry Reinhardt, president of Mills College—no other woman or ethnic minority had served, save one woman appointed for a few months in 1964 as a placeholder in the newly annexed Contra Costa County. Now, election by ward held the promise of more diverse representation.

## Master Planning

**1940**   The first general manager, Elbert M. Vail, wrote the first long-range plan for the coming decade. The District then had four regional parks: Tilden, Roundtop (Sibley), Redwood, and Temescal.

**1963**   General Manager William Penn Mott Jr. and his staff published "Forward, 1964–1969" as a detailed guide to developing user facilities at seven existing regional parks and recreation areas: Tilden, Temescal, Redwood (including Roberts), Grass Valley (later Anthony Chabot), Don Castro, Cull Canyon, and Sunol.

**1973**   Adopted by the board of directors on December 4, 1973, as Resolution No. 4475, the first of the modern-era master plans grew out of 1971 legislation (AB925) allowing the District to increase its property tax rate by ten cents, the first five-cent increase right away but the second only after adoption of a comprehensive master plan. Then-general manager Dick Trudeau took the unprecedented step of hiring former interior secretary Stewart Udall's firm, Overview, Inc., to outline technical specifications following a series of nine informational public hearings. A sixty-member Public Agency Advisory Committee and an eighty-three-member Citizens Task Force helped shape and review the draft, vetted through additional public discussion sessions and public hearings before its adoption.

   Though primarily a statement of policies for such broad areas as resources, recreation, operations, and finance, a key planning tenet specified "balanced parkland" acquisitions. Each property was to be designated a park, recreation area, wilderness, shoreline, preserve, or trail, with future or undesignated parcels to be held in land bank status.

**1980**   In 1977, the District began reviewing and revising the 1973 master plan, mainly through a subcommittee of the Park Advisory Committee. The revised version set forth further criteria for "balanced parkland" planning and equitable distribution of parklands by designating three subregions of the District: the West Metropolitan Area, the Diablo Area, and the South Metropolitan Area. The 1980 plan was adopted by the board of directors as Resolution No. 1980-2-50.

**1989** Adopted on May 17, 1988, as Resolution No. 1988-5-194, the 1989 master plan placed added emphasis on policies for resources, planning, and park operations, also codifying some longstanding District practices for the first time. This detailed plan and map became the primary documents guiding the District's first major capital bond, the $225 million Measure AA, passed by voters in November 1988.

**1997** The 1997 master plan and its associated map—the first carried out during the tenure of General Manager Pat O'Brien—represented a key planning document for the twenty-first century, setting priorities for a decade of resource conservation and management, interpretation, public access, and recreation, as well as guiding further acquisition of parkland and adding "open space" as a category of parkland, largely owing to the ongoing acquisition of the Sycamore Valley Regional Open Space Preserve. The plan stated: "An environmental ethic guides us in all that we do." It was adopted by the board of directors on December 17, 1996, as Resolution No. 1996-12-349.

**2007** The board of directors adopted the 2007 Master Plan Map, created using the latest Geographic Information System technology to identify gaps in the existing system and important natural resources needing protection. The new map, an update of the 1997 Master Plan Map, would serve to guide the creation and expansion of regional parks and trails for the next decade, as rapid urbanization would place severe limits on opportunities for new parkland acquisition.

**2009** Work began on a major revision to the master plan. As a complement to the 2007 Master Plan Map, the new document would incorporate emerging issues for the twenty-first century, such as sustainability, environmental justice, and consideration of the effects of climate change on parkland stewardship.

After joining the board in 1972, Jefferds continued her advocacy with such organizations as Save the Bay, the Audubon Society, and People for Open Space. But she consolidated much of her time and effort with the District. As the first woman board president—elected by her peers to one-year terms in 1979, 1980, and again in 1988—she became known for making frequent, if not daily, trips to the Oakland administrative headquarters on Skyline Boulevard, where a rented mobile home stood in the parking lot to serve as her office.

"She believed in a hands-on approach, instead of being a board member that recommended policy," Trudeau said. "She tried to direct the staff in how they did things."

Over time, voters began to elect fewer business leaders to represent them, while placing a new emphasis on public policy and the emerging world of environmental activism. Between elections, however, the board carried on the tradition of relying on local elected officials to suggest suitable representatives.

Shortly after Jefferds came on in 1972, Ward 4 (the cities of Alameda, San Leandro, and an inland section of Oakland) changed hands when grocer John Macdonald resigned the seat he had held since 1945. At the urging of Alameda mayor Terry La Croix, the board appointed John Leavitt, an industrial engineer, to succeed Macdonald. Reelected multiple times, Leavitt served twelve years.

Farther south, the cities of San Leandro, Hayward, Union City, and Fremont made up Ward 3, and in 1974 that seat, too, turned over. When lawyer Marlin Haley resigned, William Jardin of San Leandro's park and recreation commission was the board's choice to finish the term—also at the suggestion of his mayor, Jack Maltester—and was soon reelected, playing an early role in securing public access to the waterfront at San Leandro Bay.

In Ward 2, which started at Oakland's shoreline, spreading east through Piedmont and over the hills to Lafayette, Orinda, and Moraga, the director since 1958 was camera store owner Clyde Woolridge, also appointed by the board and then reelected. When he left in 1976, he was succeeded by Harlan Kessel.

The longtime marketing director of the University of California Press, Kessel also had amassed a distinguished record in environmental and botanical organizations, chairing the Sierra Club's publications committee for seven years and initiating a publications program for the California Native Plant Society.

By the time O'Brien became general manager late in 1988, the board often followed a pattern. Jefferds and Kessel—joined in 1987 by a new member, Kathryn Petersen, in Ward 6—often voted together as a bloc, identifying themselves as the environmentalist members. Depending upon the issue, they often voted in opposition to business owners and professionals who applied public policy skills to a more traditional community board role, such as Jim Duncan, a Kaiser executive who had represented Ward 4 since 1985, and John O'Donnell, who in 1983 had replaced Jardin in Ward 3.

Political scientist Ted Radke, representing Ward 7, and Jocelyn Combs in Ward 5 stood apart, bringing impressive environmental and public policy credentials of their own to the table. Radke had joined the Martinez City Council in his early twenties and had since racked up many victories as an environmental activist. He was now a mentor to Combs, who had sought a board vacancy in 1987 at the urging of Bob Walker, with whom she had worked on the Save Pleasanton Ridge campaign.

O'Brien saw immediately that each board member added value to the whole. With three women, the board was more diverse than ever before, but its methods had grown fuzzy, obscured by personalities, ineffective processes, and the pressure of recent events.

"When I got here, I was astounded how poorly the system actually worked," O'Brien said. "It was built for conflict."

"Getting seven people to agree on something means you have to work things out," he added. "Rather than having collision courses and then blame, you have to have systems to work out issues."

Slowly, painstakingly, O'Brien got to know each director and scrutinized the flow of ideas, staff recommendations, and other steps leading to decisions. The board's direct oversight of staff work—unheard of in most agencies—would have to stop, period.

Gradually, by laying out issues and seeking compromise well before formal votes, O'Brien defused many sources of conflict, allowing the board to work cooperatively in the appropriate role of setting policy. He genuinely enjoyed this part of his job, and it showed.

"Working with elected board members is fun to me," he said. "It's fascinating, because they're directly connected with people who vote for them."

For those directors who savored the heat of battle, he may have removed some of the thrill. The habits of the seventies and eighties, taking sides and staging the occasional boardroom showdown, had no place now. O'Brien was more interested in results than in clashes, more inclusive than adversarial, and reliably even-tempered under pressure.

Whatever the reasons, the 1990s brought a significant change of political leadership on the board. Petersen was beaten at the ballot box in 1990. Jefferds left the board in 1991 owing to ill health. Kessel let his directorship lapse, not filing for reelection in 1992 and not bothering to tell O'Brien or his board colleagues of his decision.

Board advocacy would remain a crucial element in everything the District did—an essential factor for setting policy—but the era of "conflict" advocacy as a driver of the board itself had run its course.

The remaining board members soon found new talent to fill the void. They appointed the first African-American director, Professor Carroll Williams, to complete the term of Jefferds in Ward 1, though he served only briefly before succumbing to the formidable Jean Siri at the next election.

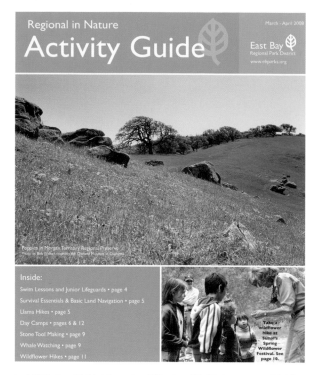

Regional in Nature
# Activity Guide

March - April 2008

East Bay
Regional Park District
www.ebparks.org

Poppies in Morgan Territory Regional Preserve

**Inside:**
Swim Lessons and Junior Lifeguards • page 4
Survival Essentials & Basic Land Navigation • page 5
Llama Hikes • page 5
Day Camps • pages 6 & 12
Stone Tool Making • page 9
Whale Watching • page 9
Wildflower Hikes • page 11

Take a wildflower hike at Sunol's Spring Wildflower Festival. See page 10.

In 1994, the District launched *Regional in Nature* as a tabloid inserted in East Bay newspapers, greatly expanding news coverage and information about interpretive and recreation programs.

Oliver Holmes won the Ward 6 seat from Kathryn Petersen. After one term he ceded his ward to former Danville mayor Beverly Lane. Certified public accountant Susan Smartt, also an accomplished parks advocate and manager at the Trust for Public Land, landed the Ward 2 seat vacated by Kessel. Environmental educator Doug Siden defeated Jim Duncan in Ward 4.

With the addition in Ward 3 of Carol Severin, a professor of recreation at San Francisco State University, the board had fully reinvented itself at the hands of voters. By 1995, stalwarts Radke and Combs had five new and highly qualified colleagues—Smartt, Siden, Siri, Lane, and Severin—whose educational and business acumen matched their substantial personal involvement with parks and the environment.

In the meantime, O'Brien had refined processes affecting the flow of information among the board, the staff, and the Park Advisory Committee. When it came to any issue, policy, or major initiative, individual board members could rely on early notification, a chance to air concerns and alternatives, good staff support, and public input from the Park Advisory Committee and their own constituents.

Simultaneous to board and bond matters, O'Brien found some practical management issues that needed attention. In 1992, he accepted the resignation of the assistant general manager of public affairs, Janet Cobb, who had been so influential in creating and passing Measure AA. Destined to assume a leadership role of her own, Cobb went on to become the executive director of the California Oak Foundation.

To fill the vacancy left by Cobb, O'Brien rehired Rosemary Cameron, the District's former legislative liaison, whom General Manager Pesonen had removed unceremoniously from the employee rolls. Cameron had substantial local government experience and had worked closely with O'Brien on the legislative committee of the California Park & Recreation Society—even, ironically, winning the society's Professional of the Year award at the very moment she was being let go by Pesonen.

Now O'Brien did not hesitate to promote her to assistant general manager of public affairs. "That was a big deal because of her capabilities to understand where I wanted to go, which was exactly what she wanted to do anyway," he said. "This whole concept of being ... a big outreach agency was right up her alley."

One change in outreach that Cameron accomplished at reasonable cost in her first years was to cease distributing the District's newsletter, *Regional Parks Log*, by mail. For years it had gone to a poorly maintained list of only 30,000 or so institutions and individuals, a list heavily weighted toward the District's visitor centers and the hill areas of Berkeley and Oakland.

"The distribution outside this elite area was limited," Cameron said.

By creating an entirely new, stand-alone supplement to area newspapers instead—modeled upon O'Brien's publication at the Southgate Recreation and Park District—the District soon reached many more constituents with a communication tool that also served as an activity guide. Starting as a quarterly, *Regional in Nature* later expanded publication to six times each year, reaching some 600,000 taxpaying citizens in both counties.

In the mid-1990s, the central department handling reservations for such amenities as group picnic areas and campsites expanded to offer registration for all classes, day camps, lessons, and other programs. Soon users could sign up or reserve by phone or through the District's full-service web site, where *Regional in Nature* also appeared.

––––––––––

Another of O'Brien's priorities during his early years was to secure enough physical space for administration. Long before he arrived, the agency had outgrown its headquarters building. Field staff were scattered in individual parks, of course, and public safety was centered near Lake Chabot. But central administrative departments occupied five different locations, limiting contact among them and fostering some balkanization of management. The finance department was at Temescal, for example, and human resources occupied rented space. Even the most routine communication was a challenge, and meetings between departments happened only with difficulty.

Before the change of general managers, the process of finding new headquarters had begun. The board had passed up a chance to locate at the new metro center in downtown Oakland, despite its proximity to public transit and other important amenities. That location would have been expensive, and some directors viewed it as too urban, not projecting the proper image for a park agency.

More recently plans had been laid to raise a new building at the current headquarters site on Skyline Boulevard. On instructions from the board, planner Mike Anderson and management chief Bob Owen had solicited wish lists from individual departments.

This building on Peralta Oaks Court near the Oakland Zoo has served as the East Bay Regional Park District's headquarters since 1992. Designed by San Francisco architect John Bolles, it was built in the mid-1960s for light industrial business use.

Architect Walter Costa, a former board member, had advised the design firm that General Manager Pesonen had retained to draw up the concept. But when O'Brien got his first look, he was taken aback at the size and scope of the proposed building, which would total some 80,000 square feet. Public affairs alone would occupy 10,000 feet.

"I had just built a community center [in Sacramento] that was 10,000 square feet," O'Brien recalled. "I said, 'Six thousand square feet is an NBA basketball court … What do we need all this space for?' It didn't make any sense."

Furthermore, the ramp in the three-story parking garage would be too narrow for two cars to pass, so a special safety rule had been devised. Drivers entering from either direction would sound their horns to warn anyone who might be headed the other way.

O'Brien found the whole arrangement a bit suspect. Some board members appeared wedded to it, though no funds had yet been raised to carry it out. There was talk of taking out a loan, but that seemed unwise, both financially and politically.

Skirting the controversy, O'Brien suggested an alternative for the immediate future, just until the new building stood ready to occupy. Since he had to manage the agency in the meantime and the staff was scattered about, might the District buy an interim building?

"When we're ready for this other building, we'll sell it," he told the board and staff. "We'll even make money. Then we'll move into the big building."

Under this plan, they began to look at locations. Taking advantage of a depressed real estate market, they bought a former manufacturing site on Peralta Oaks Court in the southern part of Oakland for just $5 million. After some $2 million in renovations to convert it to administrative use, they had spacious headquarters in a parklike setting next to Dunsmuir House and near the Oakland Zoo.

The interim building, occupied beginning in March 1992, served its purpose so well that the plan to build at Skyline fell by the wayside. Later, the District did remodel the Skyline building, converting two existing levels to serve as a training

Constructed in 1868 when Temescal Creek was dammed to create a reservoir, Lake Temescal opened to the public in 1936 as one of the first three East Bay regional parks. The lakeside stone building, built by Works Progress Administration crews, served as the District's headquarters building until the 1960s.

center. Though modest in scope compared to the sizable structure that had once been proposed there, the project drew substantial opposition from neighbors and open space advocates.

"We could never have built anything new there, to tell you the truth," O'Brien said. "The City of Oakland was siding with the neighbors. It was very difficult."

The consolidation of administrative functions to a single building represented more than an increase of space or a change of location. Through that seemingly innocuous adjustment to the District's basic setup, O'Brien effected a sea change of sorts.

"It was probably one of the least recognized but actually more significant things we've done," O'Brien said, "to consolidate administration so that we could work together more as a team."

In a public agency with fifty-plus years of fascinating and complex history, working as a team could never be taken for granted. By consolidating and professionalizing the look and feel of the administrative work space, O'Brien had taken an important step toward that larger, more important goal.

This north-facing aerial view showcases the 8.5-mile linear Eastshore State Park, which extends from the Bay Bridge and the Emeryville crescent (foreground) to Richmond.

## Chapter 7

# Shoreline

*The most important resource in California today, in the world, and in any civilization, is water.*

—JOHN NEJEDLY, former state senator, 1982

Nearly twenty years after the fact, Esther Gulick could recall the evening of January 7, 1969, when she turned on the television in her Berkeley home to watch news coverage of Governor Ronald Reagan's "State of the State" address. Just starting his third year as California's chief executive, Reagan had every reason to exude confidence. The Democrats' powerhouse assembly speaker of the past seven years, Jesse Unruh, had stepped down only the day before, yielding to Republican victories in the November 1968 election, a contest that would also, in a matter of weeks, see Richard M. Nixon sworn in as the nation's thirty-seventh president.

Reagan's speech promised Californians a balanced budget and an income tax reduction before calling for legislation to curb the threats of "anarchy and insurrection" embodied in recent demonstrations on college campuses around the state.

Distracted for a moment from her television, Gulick suddenly realized that the governor had also addressed the subject of San Francisco Bay. He appeared to have spoken favorably, even calling the bay "a priceless natural resource."

Gulick was flabbergasted.

"We were worried about Governor Reagan," she said later. "Most of his support, financial and otherwise, came from Southern California, and he was not known for his interest in the environment."

Though not particularly moved by such things himself, Governor Reagan did have in his cabinet two appointees with a serious interest in protecting the glorious estuary made up of the inland Sacramento-San Joaquin Delta and San Francisco Bay. One was

The founders of Save the Bay are (from top) Kay Kerr, Esther Gulick, and Sylvia McLaughlin.

Secretary of Resources Norman "Ike" Livermore Jr., and the other was Director of Finance Caspar Weinberger.

Furthermore, one of the resource departments under Livermore's purview was State Parks and Recreation, whose director, William Penn Mott Jr., had served as general manager of the East Bay Regional Park District from 1962 to 1967. The duo of Livermore and Mott, Reagan biographer Lou Cannon wrote, "gave the Reagan administration a conservationist stance that neither friend nor foe had anticipated."

By the time of Reagan's speech, Gulick, Kay Kerr, and Sylvia McLaughlin had been at work for nine years to halt filling of the bay—which had lost nearly 30 percent of its area since the Gold Rush—and to save tidal marshlands from further destruction. Inspired by a set of "before and after" U.S. Army Corps of Engineers maps foretelling a dire future for the bay, they had founded the Save San Francisco Bay Association ("Save the Bay") in their living rooms. By the end of 1962, they had 2,500 members.

From his seat in the state assembly, Nicholas Petris had helped them raise awareness of threats to the bay. While his early protection bills did not pass, they set the stage for legislation in 1964 by a powerful state senator, Eugene McAteer, to create the San Francisco Bay Conservation Study Commission. The commission's report in turn provided a stepping stone for the McAteer-Petris Act of 1965, which created the Bay Conservation and Development Commission (BCDC). After losing Senator McAteer to a heart attack in 1967, the fledgling bay conservation movement had—just days before Governor Reagan's "State of the State" speech—learned of the sudden death by heart attack of another champion in the state legislature, Senator George Miller, on New Year's Day, 1969.

Transferring the mantle of advocacy to Assemblyman Jack Knox, BCDC and its supporters had sent a plan to the governor and the legislature to justify and urge the commission's continued existence. As state parks director, Mott could exert a particular influence. Indeed, while managing the East Bay Regional Park District he had simultaneously served as president of Save the Bay's board. Even so, environmentalists were astonished at the governor's apparent willingness to give them political cover.

"There was great surprise when Reagan, in his 'State of the State' message, came out for a continuation of BCDC," Gulick said. "After Reagan supported the bay, the issue in the legislature became bipartisan."

## Bay Conservation and Development Commission

The San Francisco Bay Conservation and Development Commission (BCDC) is a California state commission created by the McAteer-Petris Act of 1965 and serving as the federally-designated state coastal management agency for the San Francisco Bay segment of the California coastal zone. In the early 1960s, Assemblyman Nicholas Petris had aided the Save San Francisco Bay Association ("Save the Bay") in sounding early warnings of threats to San Francisco Bay, which had lost some 30 percent of its area since the Gold Rush to landfill. His early attempts at legislation set the stage for a powerful state senator, Eugene McAteer, to engineer the creation of the San Francisco Bay Conservation Study Commission and then, later, the permanent commission itself.

*Making San Francisco Bay Better*

Completed in January 1969, the San Francisco Bay Plan set forth policies for use of the bay, providing detailed maps to designate shoreline areas for specific water-related purposes such as ports, industry, public recreation, airports, and wildlife refuges. In August 1969, the McAteer-Petris Act was amended to make BCDC a permanent agency and to incorporate the policies of the San Francisco Bay Plan into state law. Since 1977 the commission's authority has extended to protection of Suisun Marsh.

Administered for many years by Executive Director Will Travis, the commission consists of 27 members, five of them (including the chairman and vice-chairman) appointed by the governor, four appointed by the Association of Bay Area Governments, and one each appointed by the assembly speaker, the Senate Rules Committee, the boards of supervisors of each of the nine Bay Area counties, the Business and Transportation Agency, the Department of Finance, the Resources Agency, the State Lands Commission, the Regional Water Quality Control Board, the U. S. Army Corps of Engineers, and the U. S. Environmental Protection Agency.

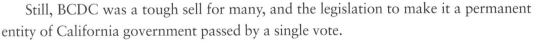

Still, BCDC was a tough sell for many, and the legislation to make it a permanent entity of California government passed by a single vote.

Meanwhile, the East Bay Regional Park District had for some years planned to "go to the water" in future park acquisitions to complement the significant existing acreage on and near the hills. The general desirability of shoreline parks was heightened by the rising issue of inadequate public access to the waterfront. Nearly the entire eastern edge of the bay—a length of nearly one hundred miles—rested in private hands, much of it given over to industrial uses.

This north-facing image of Point Pinole Regional Shoreline highlights the beauty of undeveloped shoreline near an urbanized area.

During Mott's tenure as general manager, the master plan had included the goal to acquire Point Pinole in western Contra Costa County. Jutting into San Pablo Bay midway between the cities of Pinole and Richmond, Point Pinole included four miles of rocky cliff shoreline and abundant low-lying tidal marshlands. Bethlehem Steel had bought the property after the old Atlas Powder Company ceased manufacturing gunpowder there in 1960, but few local citizens had seen it with their own eyes.

In the throes of annexing Contra Costa County to the District, Mott became convinced that he should remove Point Pinole from his acquisition plans for the time being, owing to the City of Richmond's objections, while maintaining an unofficial goal to try for it later. Sure enough, Bethlehem Steel backed off its own plan to develop the land and appeared ready to negotiate. As Mott's right hand for administration and public relations, Dick Trudeau was alerted to the possible sale by the Urban Land Institute and worked alongside the District's land chief, Hulet Hornbeck, to obtain an option to buy Point Pinole.

Meanwhile, Mott and the District's board—especially the stockbroker member, Fred Blumberg—urged Bethlehem to sell and arranged a low-interest loan of $3 million from Bank of America, the first significant loan the District had ever sought to buy land.

The long process of acquiring Point Pinole continued after Trudeau succeeded Mott as general manager in 1968. After establishing a foothold by leasing modest acreage there from the State Lands Commission—a parcel abutting the residential development known as Parchester Village—the District finally arranged in 1973 to purchase a thousand acres from Bethlehem in two phases. Coming to agreement on price, however, proved arduous, and the District "lost it three times in negotiations" before finally striking a workable deal.

Much of the groundwork to "Save Point Pinole" was laid through the efforts of the East Bay's environmental power couple, Will and Jean Siri of El Cerrito. A biophysicist and legendary mountaineer who also had served as national president of the Sierra Club, Will Siri addressed the question of Point Pinole from behind the scenes, quietly and unofficially lobbying the president of Bethlehem Steel to consider selling land to create a regional park.

As a leading light of Save the Bay since its inception, Jean Siri took a different approach. With Point Pinole's future up for grabs, she rallied supporters to openly and vocally oppose development of the land by Bethlehem or by the City of Richmond, which had taken a strong pro-development stance in hopes of generating revenue.

Even further behind the scenes, Hulet Hornbeck was sworn to keep Will Siri's "under the radar" negotiations a secret from his own wife. "If it had gotten out that he was talking to Bethlehem Steel, it would have stopped the deal," Bob Doyle said later. Jean Siri, as everyone on the staff knew, was not to be trifled with. "She was calling Hulet probably every other day and hounding him," Doyle said, "and she could really hound people."

Although Jean Siri would not join the District's board of directors until 1993—serving with distinction until her death in 2006—many players credit her with the District's success in acquiring Point Pinole.

By combining the bank loan with a federal Land and Water Conservation grant and a quarter-million-dollar gift from the Whitell Foundation, the District convinced its own Public Agency Advisory Committee and separate Citizens Task Force—nearly 150 people in all—to recommend acquiring Point Pinole immediately rather than waiting for the new master plan. Unless they acted soon, the right conditions might never again materialize.

As the largest undeveloped piece of bay shoreline, Point Pinole needed only minimal amenities to become a magnet for fishing, family cycling, and birding. One of the first full-time rangers there, Bob Doyle, recalled the pleasure of spending time in the remote reaches of the new park.

"It really is a miracle that [the property] was not lost," he said. "Everybody assumes you always hit home runs . . . but I can't believe they got a large upland parcel alongside a significant undeveloped shoreline. It's a rare combination."

With Point Pinole in the bag, local activists such as Jean Siri and Lucretia Edwards helped the District add acreage to other waterfront parks in keeping with its new master plan of 1973. The first was Miller/Knox Regional Shoreline at Point Richmond, the

Jean Siri represented Ward 1 on the park district's board from 1992 until her death in 2006.

former western terminus of the Transcontinental Railroad, where arriving passengers could catch the ferry to San Francisco from 1900 to 1975.

Although the District had acquired 53 acres from Santa Fe Railway in 1970, most of the 300-acre park came in small parcels after 1975. Named for Assemblyman Jack Knox and the late Senator George Miller, the scenic waterfront stood in serious disrepair when the District's staff set to work preparing it for use as a park. By investing in a lengthy cleanup process, they could provide a beautiful and safe site for fishing, swimming, birding, and hiking, including the steep trek to the top of 371-foot Nicholl Knob, with its panoramic view.

"That's an example of turning an industrial area into a park," said General Manager Pat O'Brien. "When you're done, people just think it's natural."

As an equity issue—even before the phrase "environmental justice" came into common use—O'Brien and his staff saw no reason the Richmond side of the bay shouldn't be as beautiful and as usable as its counterpart in Marin County. As an economic reality, residents on the two sides of the bay might lead very different lives, but they had the same need for outdoor beauty and family recreation as people anywhere. After all, the east and west shorelines had once been nearly identical.

"There's no difference between the bay side of the Marin shoreline and the Richmond shoreline except what was built on it," O'Brien said. "It has almost the same climate and the same physical characteristics."

Just a few miles south, the District also established Point Isabel Regional Shoreline, which it operated by leasing the property since 1975 from the U.S. Postal Service. Again, the land, planning, and operations departments had to factor in extensive cleanup, mitigation of previous industrial use, and restoration of the dynamic marshlands native to that part of the bay shore.

The newly developed Point Isabel had few users at first, so the District designated certain lawns and picnic areas for people who wished to enjoy the waterfront with off-leash dogs. In 1985 a group of canine enthusiasts formed the nonprofit Point Isabel Dog Owners and Friends to help maintain the canine section of the park by educating visitors and supplying "mutt mitts" for waste disposal.

Farther south in Alameda County, the District devised one of its most creative shoreline parks in a tightly packed industrial area anchored by the Port of Oakland. Starting in the mid-sixties, a core group of advocates—including John Sutter, who would join the Oakland City Council and, later, the District's board—had pressured port authorities to stop filling the bay and allow public access to the waterfront.

"It took years, but we just kept working on them," Sutter said.

When public access at last became a reality, the 741-acre park opened in 1979 as the San Leandro Bay Regional Shoreline. Although the Port of Oakland still owned most of the land circling the small bay, adjacent to both Oakland International Airport

A mere twenty-three acres in size, Point Isabel Regional Shoreline (shown here with the Golden Gate Bridge in the distance) is the largest public off-leash dog park in the nation, attracting more than 500,000 dog visits per year.

and the professional sports stadium known as the Coliseum, the District entered into a unique arrangement to build the park and to lease and operate it with participation and approval from the Bay Conservation and Development Commission.

More than a decade later, community leader Ira Jinkins consulted with the District's planning chief, Mike Anderson, about adding a grove of trees in memory of Dr. Martin Luther King Jr. Jinkins also voiced his hope that a community center would one day be built in the park to carry on Dr. King's teachings. Although the tree grove qualified for a small urban forestry grant, awards could be made only on land owned outright or leased for twenty-five years or longer.

After the Port of Oakland refused to extend the lease, an even better idea arose. General Manager O'Brien and the board's San Leandro representative, Jim Duncan, tried it out on Oakland mayor Elihu Harris.

"What if the entire park at San Leandro Bay was renamed for Dr. King?" they asked.

Harris's enthusiastic response echoed throughout the community, and in 1992, the board—in spite of opposition by its own Park Advisory Committee—voted unanimously to rename the San Leandro Bay Regional Shoreline. Ira Jinkins, Assemblywoman (now

Congresswoman) Barbara Lee, and other honored guests helped rededicate the park as the Martin Luther King Jr. Regional Shoreline. The District added the memorial grove with community support in 1993.

The park represented a triumph of effort by local citizens, in partnership with the District and the Port of Oakland, to offer rare open space shoreline access in the midst of an industrial urban area. The arrangement also protected the fifty-acre tidal Arrowhead Marsh, a stopover on the Pacific Flyway that makes up a part of the Western Hemisphere Shorebird Reserve Network.

After the name change, Lee and the East Oakland community revived Jinkins's idea to create a regional center dedicated to "Dr. King's ideals of nonviolence, social change, racial and economic justice, and a peaceful world." The Martin Luther King Jr. Freedom Center—formed under a joint agreement between the District, the City of Oakland, the Port of Oakland, the California Coastal Conservancy, and the Martin Luther King Jr. March and Rally Committee—established its offices in the shoreline center at the park. Doug Siden, who succeeded Jim Duncan on the District's board, served on the center's board as well.

Many other shoreline and island parks would join the District's territory over the years, several of them fanning out to the east along the inland delta. Creation of the Martinez Regional Shoreline, which had appeared in the master plan since the 1970s, led eventually to acquisition of both the Carquinez Regional Shoreline and the nearby Crockett Hills Regional Park.

Although the District had a record of creative joint projects, none was so challenging as the collaboration with the State of California to establish Eastshore State Park, a publicly accessible section of the eastern bayshore between Richmond and Oakland.

When the Santa Fe Railway moved in 1971 to develop a massive shopping center— a million square feet—on land it owned at the Berkeley waterfront, nearby cities already had created substantial landfill from garbage or construction materials during the long history of the waterfront, which stretched back many decades. Indeed, the founders of Save the Bay had organized in opposition to a host of similar threats to the bay's integrity, many of them from the cities themselves.

This time, however, the City of Berkeley joined citizen activists to oppose the development. Santa Fe filed a lawsuit charging inverse condemnation, a dispute that carried on until 1980, when the California Supreme Court ruled in Berkeley's favor for the tidal area, remanding the land portion of the lawsuit for further review before dismissing it altogether.

Meanwhile, no landfill could occur without a permit from the Bay Conservation and Development Commission, and in time the commission flexed enough muscle to halt that particular project for good. Santa Fe grew more ambitious still, drawing up new plans to build millions of commercial square feet on the waterfront. The affected communities of Albany, Berkeley, Emeryville, and Oakland began the arduous process of reviewing and voting upon these latest designs.

Spurred by a 1980 proposal from Save the Bay and the Sierra Club to form a sizable waterfront park instead, Assemblyman Tom Bates approached state authorities about acquiring the property and creating Eastshore State Park. The idea had appeared in the Bay Conservation and Development Commission's first "bay plan" of the late 1960s, but the questions of ownership and management had never been worked out. The state park bond act of 1976 included seed funds for an Eastshore park. The state parks department conducted a feasibility study in 1982, while the Coastal Conservancy began a planning process that confirmed strong public support for the concept.

Retired New York Yankees baseball star Joe DiMaggio (third from left), a native of Martinez, threw out the first pitch on the softball diamond at the Martinez Regional Shoreline dedication ceremony. Other celebrants included (from left) board members Harlan Kessel, Ted Radke, Mary Jefferds, Bill Jardin, and Dr. Howard Cogswell and outgoing board member Paul Badger.

The proposed park did appear on the state parks project list, but in the early years of Governor George Deukmejian's administration—even with political pressure to "get out of the redwoods" and provide urban parks that were readily accessible to taxpayers—the agency never managed to acquire any property.

While Bates continued to work the halls at the Capitol, a coalition of environmental organizations—including Save the Bay, the Sierra Club, the Golden Gate Audubon Society, Urban Care, the League of Women Voters, and several shoreline groups—consolidated their efforts by forming Citizens for Eastshore State Park in 1985. Started by Save the Bay cofounder Sylvia McLaughlin and Dwight Steele, and with individuals such as Mary Jefferds and Norman La Force in the vanguard, the fledgling group organized to thwart further efforts at developing the shoreline for commercial purposes and to advocate for creation of the state park.

Although progress toward that goal was slow and fraught with controversy, by 1990 residents of Berkeley, Albany, and Emeryville had passed ballot measures to protect the remaining open space on the shoreline. In 1988, the California Parks and Wildlife Act, passed by voters as Proposition 70, included $25 million toward acquiring the lands for Eastshore.

Santa Fe Railway had reorganized, creating a separate land development arm, Catellus Corporation, that now owned the property. After the cities voted to protect the waterfront, Catellus could not develop its land. But it might be persuaded to sell, and by 1992, with no real action forthcoming from the state, Assemblyman Bates switched tactics, approaching the District about the possibility of becoming involved.

"He was going to run a bill to transfer the authority to the East Bay Regional Park District to be the lead in the acquisition and planning and development of Eastshore State Park," General Manager O'Brien recalled. "He had a lot of confidence that we could do it."

But the unorthodox collaboration and the financial complexity of the proposed arrangement made it a lightning rod with the board and staff. With the state mired in a fiscal crisis, which could translate to a significant loss of operating funds, did the District really want to venture into creating a state park? O'Brien understood the reluctance, and he agreed that Eastshore represented a planning nightmare, but his view of the larger picture was different. To avoid or at least minimize local property tax transfers, which the state was employing to balance its budget, the District would need ongoing support from Bates and his colleagues.

"Several of our board members did not want this state park project," O'Brien said. "I remember telling them, 'I'd rather figure out how to do a park than figure out how to cut our budget.'"

Once Bates's hard-fought legislation passed, making the District a state agent for creating Eastshore, the state parks department and the District, led by land chief Bob Doyle, began negotiating with Catellus Corporation to buy the property. Funds had been painstakingly pieced together from two 1988 bond measures, statewide Proposition 70 and the District's own Measure AA, as well as other state and local sources.

As the purchase effort unfolded, it became clear that Governor Pete Wilson's secretary of resources, Doug Wheeler, had bigger plans, of which Eastshore was but one part. When the District sought an independent appraisal of the property's value, Wheeler intervened to promote a private appraisal obtained by Catellus.

"I appreciated his viewpoint," O'Brien said, "but we waited to see the results of the independent appraisal."

Coming in much lower, the new appraisal may have threatened to weaken Wheeler's bargaining position for acquiring parklands from Catellus on a grander scale elsewhere in California.

"His proposed sale would have used all available funds, which was about $90 million," O'Brien said. "I'm sure, from his perspective, he had a great environmental deal in the making as part of a larger state acquisition priority, but that wasn't our focus."

"Any two agencies are going to have different focuses and different priorities," he added. "Maybe if I was working on a much bigger deal, that might have made perfect sense. But it certainly didn't make sense to us in terms of what we were doing at Eastshore."

Also, while the District never used its power of condemnation until other means had been exhausted, it was prepared to take that step in order to provide parks for taxpaying constituents. In contrast, the state was unlikely to invoke eminent domain to create a park. The state

California State Parks Director Don Murphy and Assemblyman Tom Bates announce at a press conference along the shoreline in Emeryville the completed initial acquisition of Eastshore State Park, 889 acres that included the Emeryville crescent in Oakland, the Albany mudflats and shoreline, and the Hoffman Marsh in Richmond, all of which preserve important wetlands and critical wildlife habitat. In 1992, Bates authored AB754, which designated the East Bay Regional Park District as the state's agent for acquiring, planning, and developing the park.

transportation agency, Caltrans, might condemn for a highway now and then, but for a park such state action was unlikely.

"That was another reason Tom Bates wanted us to get involved, because he knew we could have that hammer to press for an acquisition," O'Brien said. "We ended up buying this property for $27.5 million instead of $90 million. That was within the independent appraisal and with a threat of condemnation."

The threat alone—the stated intent to convert the land to public use under the right of eminent domain—proved sufficient, and no actual condemnation occurred.

"We got quite a bit . . . for $27.5 million," O'Brien said, "but the state was not happy with us."

"It isn't that they're wrong or we're right, it's just we have one objective and they have a different objective," he added. "Wheeler wanted to acquire Eastshore State Park, too. He just wanted to acquire it at a higher price as part of a larger package."

As the project progressed, the District—in cooperation with the state and with Citizens for Eastshore State Park and other advocacy groups—led a massive public planning effort. A series of public forums outstripped all expectations, drawing 3,000 citizens who participated in discussions to piece together a common vision for the proposed park and communicate it to elected officials. The citizen participation process later won park planning awards.

Among the District's staff, the planning and mitigation sapped significant time and resources.

"We did 1,500 borings of the landfill to convince the state that it was not leaking into the bay," said Doyle.

But the results were stellar. Eastshore State Park opened in a limited capacity in 1997, a living testament to the vision set forth by a few and three decades of work by many.

In December 2002, the California State Park and Recreation Commission gave unanimous approval to the general plan for establishing Eastshore as a state park under a joint operating agreement with the District. The new park opened in 2006 to its full length of 8.5 miles, from the Richmond marina to the Bay Bridge in Oakland. By preserving more than 2,000 acres of tidelands and 250 acres of uplands, it provided critical habitat for sixteen species of rare, threatened, or endangered wildlife. It also added a substantial segment to the San Francisco Bay Trail, one that otherwise might never have materialized.

The difficult and years-long acquisition, mitigation, and eventual operation of Eastshore State Park taught the District to think in new ways about the importance of citizen participation in achieving results. The new park represented a pivotal philosophical lesson that would continue to guide the board and staff.

"We learned so much by our leadership on Eastshore that it has left a permanent mark on the District's willingness to take on difficult urban projects," said Doyle, the land chief. "We have a duty to create parks where people need them."

The Point Pinole area returned to the spotlight in 2000 when the nearby 238-acre Breuner Marsh sold to a private company that aimed to resell it for development. A large wetland habitat for threatened and endangered species such as the clapper rail and the salt marsh harvest mouse, Breuner Marsh had no equal among privately held lands anywhere in the East Bay. All comparable wetlands had either won protection or disappeared.

Zoned "light industrial" by the City of Richmond, the marsh had come to the District's attention much earlier through residents of nearby Parchester Village. As an addition to the existing Point Pinole Regional Shoreline, Breuner Marsh would provide limited public access—and a critical link in the San Francisco Bay Trail—while also offering the chance to restore the marshland and protect wildlife habitat. But as a difficult acquisition with no clear window of opportunity, it had remained out of reach and threatened.

Now, local activists saw a dire need to fight development but also a chance to preserve the marsh as open space. At their urging, the District approached the new owner.

Bay Area Wetlands LLC responded by announcing plans for imminent development, part of which would encroach on the marsh itself. After sustained efforts to purchase the property, the District initiated a condemnation in order to acquire it by eminent domain.

Breuner Marsh, acquired by the East Bay Regional Park District in 2008 with strong support from residents of Parchester Village in Richmond, will undergo significant restoration work on about 100 acres of wetlands and grasslands that provide habitat for endangered or rare plants and animals such as the California clapper rail.

"It became clear that we probably were not going to be able to protect that property, or even a sizable chunk of it, through negotiations," O'Brien said.

"It became, really, an environmental justice issue for us," he added. "We wanted to provide wildlife protection, and we wanted to provide habitat protection, but we wanted to provide public access for this community. The only way we were going to get that was to go to court."

Residents of Parchester Village had grown up having unofficial access to Breuner Marsh. Now they felt strongly that the area should remain an open space. As land chief, Doyle witnessed their pleas at District board meetings. "They would be in tears, begging us to protect the shoreline they loved," he said.

The City of Richmond, however, had other ideas. Viewing the marsh as a potential source of revenue, it adopted a pro-development stance—"bullish, one might say," as O'Brien put it—and the various parties could not come to terms.

Following condemnation and a protracted court battle, the District's purchase of Breuner Marsh was at last allowed to proceed at a price of $6.85 million, an amount chosen by jury that fell between the appraised value of $1.5 million and the $18 million

Big Break Regional Shoreline, located in Oakley (Contra Costa County) on the San Joaquin River, is being developed in phases. The future Delta Discovery Experience and Delta Science Center will offer environmental education programs here focusing on the sensitive California Delta, the largest estuarine environment on the Pacific Coast.

claimed by the owner. Though most of the property would be protected, the District had to concede twenty-five upland acres to the City of Richmond for possible development at some later time.

But even with a few imperfections, Breuner Marsh ranked high on the District's list of hard-fought but worthwhile acquisitions. With this victory—building upon the lessons of Eastshore—the board and staff had again stepped up to the plate in the hardball world of land deals and hit one out, as it were, saving in perpetuity an exceedingly rare piece of shoreline.

Today the bay and its protected shores stand as living testament to the contributions of Esther Gulick and her sister visionaries, as well as the citizen activists who followed them. San Francisco Bay enjoys protective advocacy from Save the Bay, Citizens for Eastshore State Park, and other nonprofit organizations, while the Bay Conservation and Development Commission provides regulatory oversight and the Coastal Conservancy supplies essential grant funding.

Under protection of the East Bay Regional Park District, the public now has access to nearly fifty miles of shoreline in Alameda and Contra Costa counties. More than a dozen waterfront parks line the bay's eastern shore and the inland delta, including the Carquinez Strait, Martinez, and Antioch Regional Shorelines, Browns Island, and Big Break, which extends public waterfront access as far east as Oakley.

The District's strategic management and enhancement of resources—much of it exploiting cutting-edge technology—reaches far beyond those first urgent calls to save San Francisco Bay and to scrutinize every mile of its shoreline. The activists of the 1960s could hardly have imagined that their success would be carried forward through programs of stewardship that operate as if the future of waterfront open space is and will be assured.

It took many years, but in facing the rough-and-tumble realities where the water meets the shore, the District's board and staff mastered a surprisingly simple lesson.

In addition to offering a lovely site for citizens to enjoy the waterfront, the Martin Luther King Jr. Regional Shoreline includes a segment of the San Francisco Bay Trail (shown at left) and protects the remainder of a once-extensive marshland and bird habitat at San Leandro Bay.

In the sophisticated and densely populated East Bay, good intentions and good management alone would not bring excellent results. Every waterfront park created since the master plan of 1973—some of them decades in the making—had roots in general voter approval at the ballot box, and every one took shape through the essential push of citizen advocacy.

Only through the democratic process, thorns and all, could the bay and delta shores beckon as they do today, inviting the public into accessible open spaces with abundant wildlife. The active participation of ordinary citizens, combined with the District's know-how in using politics and law to advantage, has worked small miracles for future generations. Now and forever the East Bay's millions can, as never before, go to the water.

This robust young coyote at Round Valley Regional Preserve is tangible evidence of the East Bay Regional Park District's comprehensive approach to acquiring and managing open space. The board and staff seek to provide adequate and safe public access to parks while actively protecting wildlife and native habitat.

## Chapter 8

# Stewardship

*Invasive species are one of the most serious environmental problems of the twenty-first century. They crowd out native species, disrupt natural processes, and impose tremendous costs on human communities. This is even more true for California than for most other states in the country.*

—*Weed Workers' Handbook*, a publication of the Watershed Project and the California Invasive Plant Council, 2004

Outside the main building at Temescal Regional Recreation Area, supervisor Frances Heath stood quite alone on Sunday morning, October 20, 1991, and watched as flames swallowed the skyline and steadily consumed the western flank of the Oakland hills. The fire was burning ever closer to her park, and this lakeside building, though crafted of stone in the 1930s, had a shake roof.

Without waiting for official guidance or help of any kind, Heath yanked manual water sprinklers from the supply shed and wrestled them onto the building's wood shingles. She turned on the water, and for the rest of the morning she soaked the roof, wetting as much as she could of the surrounding area with a hose. When the Oakland command post relocated to Temescal and fire crews arrived, her solo stand was over.

By noon Heath saw the conflagration jump Highway 24, raining firebrands down onto Temescal trees. In a high, shifting wind, the hot spots passed quickly over the lake and main buildings, feasting instead on the west hillside and the homes beyond. Flare-ups within the park continued, and soon only blackened earth remained as evidence of an old groundskeeper's cottage, along with an unmistakable smell. But the beach house and other buildings stood intact.

The East Bay Regional Park District's fire department uses a variety of methods to reduce hazardous wildland fuels, maintain fuel breaks in the East Bay hills, and control invasive weeds. Here firefighters light a prescribed burn near the Seaview Trail in Tilden Regional Park to reduce hazardous fuels from eucalyptus duff. Prescribed fires have other benefits, including improving wildlife habitat, managing competing vegetation, perpetuating fire-dependent native plant species, and improving access and aesthetic values.

Among other things, the controller's office—with the safe and all of the East Bay Regional Park District's financial records—had been spared. As District managers Jerry Kent and Steve Jones approached, Heath walked forward, arms folded across her chest.

"Well, boys," she said, "I saved your paychecks."

While destroying most vegetation at Temescal, the East Bay Hills firestorm of October 1991 burned through part of Claremont Canyon too. Firefighters and the field staff managed to limit the damage to structures and park resources, but cleanup costs later exceeded $500,000.

The East Bay as a whole suffered an incalculable loss that could later be reduced to tidy numbers: twenty-five lives lost, three square miles burned, 2,900 homes ravaged, and more than $1.5 billion in damages. A product of "Diablo winds" from the east, this fire was the worst urban blaze in California since at least the start of reliable recordkeeping in the 1920s. Even the Berkeley fire of 1923 offered no comparison.

The District had emphasized fire prevention throughout its history, owing in part to the risk inherent in the East Bay topography. Even the first three parks, opened in 1936, had great geographic variety, rising from near sea level to 2,000 feet in a mix of steep and gentle slopes with both north- and south-flowing streams.

Though redwoods dominated in gulches draining into the northern end of San Leandro Reservoir, most tree cover consisted of live oak, California bay laurel, buckeye, and madrone, with smaller stands of alder and willow. The early parklands also featured nonnative trees such as cypress, Monterey pine, and eucalyptus. On the upper slopes, serpentine grasslands prevailed, studded with coyote brush, poison oak, and sage.

"Records kept since 1926 indicate clearly the ever-present fire threat to which the area is subject," reads the General Fire Plan commissioned by the District in 1936. The Contra Costa Hills Fire Prevention Committee, organized in 1922, had established two lookout stations on Grizzly and Roundtop peaks, the report stated, but these and other efforts had been inadequately funded by the twenty committee members, which included cities, public utilities, park departments, safety and hiking organizations, and the University of California. The City of Berkeley and the East Bay Municipal Utility District had contributed an appropriate share of the financing, the report continued, but "unfortunately the City of Oakland does not appreciate the need for their material assistance and co-operation in the committee's activities."

---

The East Bay Regional Park District would in time grow to ten times its original size in square miles, continuing to place priority on cutting-edge public safety techniques and on coordinating with the police and fire departments of cities and other entities. By 1973, with 1,300 square miles to patrol, the board authorized purchase of a helicopter, which greatly aided the District's ability to prevent major problems on a regional scale. Later, a backup helicopter added an additional capacity to prevent and respond to fires and other emergencies across a growing area of responsibility.

The expanding territory included a great variety of landscapes, climatic variations, and natural cycles. The eucalyptus, for example, regularly froze and died off when winter temperatures ran low enough, only to sprout vigorous new growth in spring that served as plentiful and efficient fuel for wildfires.

The much-maligned eucalyptus had earned special condemnation from Jim Roof, the first director of Tilden Regional Park's botanic garden. Calling them "horrible water suckers," Roof noted that they concentrate moisture under their canopy, leading to thickets of blackberries, poison oak, ivy, and wild cucumber. "The end result is the rendering of once open, sunny, wildflower-bearing land into foreboding and pestilential jungles of no earthly use to man, bird, or beast," he wrote.

In the aftermath of an extraordinary eucalyptus freeze early in 1972, then-General Manager Dick Trudeau traveled to Washington, D.C., to seek $15 million in federal aid. Senator Alan Cranston introduced legislation to fund cleanup of the damage and help prevent future wildfires by replacing eucalyptus with native trees.

When a congressman from Idaho, Steve Sims, came to California to have a look for himself, he was unmoved by what he saw. Returning to Washington, he adopted a slogan of opposition on the floor of the House to sound like the word eucalyptus. "You clipped us!" he cried. The bill failed by only thirty-four votes. The District later won $2 million from another federal program to carry out a scaled-back replacement of fuel breaks and nonnative trees, also taking special precautions during the following fire season.

Trudeau paid close attention to matters of fire safety over his years as general manager. At his urging, the board of directors in 1981 fulfilled the request of El Cerrito mayor Margaret Collins and appointed a Blue Ribbon Urban Interface Fire Prevention

Committee. Trudeau enlisted William Penn Mott Jr., the former leader of both the District and the state Department of Parks and Recreation, to chair the twenty-seven-member committee of local government representatives and University of California scientists who would "study the fire danger in the East Bay hills between natural lands and the urbanized residential areas."

Filing a 100-page report in February 1982, the committee suggested a three-step plan for minimizing the risk of fire at the interface of the urban and wildland zones. First, the report would be distributed to all affected entities, which would then meet with committee members seeking formal support of the regional effort. Second, agencies would conduct public hearings throughout the interface zone to conform with guidelines of the California Environmental Quality Act and to inform area residents. Finally, a joint powers agency for affected cities and agencies would develop a final construction and action plan, with the recommendation that a special assessment district be created to fund fuel breaks and other prevention projects.

Assistant General Manager Jerry Kent and Rosemary Cameron, two of the five District representatives, became intimately involved in the research, planning, and writing of the report.

"We included many important details, but at that time we did not recognize the full power of Diablo winds," Kent recalled.

Although the affected cities and agencies did adopt the regional plan, the joint powers agency never materialized and the implementation phase was not fully realized. As time passed, the urgent message of the report—coordinated prevention for the region—began to fade.

Within the District, General Manager Pat O'Brien and the board of directors upheld and expanded upon Trudeau's legacy of preventive public safety, insisting upon the latest technology and the best equipment for a staff trained to fight wildland fires. In October 1991, nearly ten years after the Blue Ribbon committee completed its work, a small crew of District firefighters helped the Oakland Fire Department extinguish a Saturday fire that reignited the next morning to become the devastating East Bay hills firestorm.

Summoned to the site on Sunday morning to retrieve their fire hose, five District employees, all experienced wildland firefighters, instead reconnected the hose in the face of new flare-ups. They stayed on, fighting for hours alongside city and state fire departments as the shifting Diablo winds wreaked their havoc upon the hills.

In the aftermath of the deadly firestorm, cities and agencies renewed the regional fire prevention effort for the East Bay. As a founding member of the Hills Emergency Forum

## Bicycles in the East Bay Regional Parks

Bicyclists have long been enthusiastic users of the parks and trails of the East Bay Regional Park District, as well as important constituents to consider in park planning. The rising popularity of mountain biking beginning in the 1980s required the District to address service to cyclists while protecting parkland and ensuring fair and safe use by others.

By 1987, the board had taken a hard look at mountain biking and decided to limit cyclists to fire roads on the 65,000 or so hilly park acres. Two years later, the *Wall Street Journal* reported on the phenomenon of mountain biking, which was changing the experience of the outdoors at the District and everywhere else.

"When the [mountain] bikes first entered mass production in 1981, they were dismissed as a trend," the *Journal* wrote. "Last year [1988], 25 percent of the 10 million bicycles sold in the U.S. were mountain bikes. In California, a bellwether market, they accounted for more than 80 percent of all bike sales."

Since that initial growth spurt, the "fat tire" community has become an important presence in a society concerned with recreation, transportation, and the environment. On District lands, cyclists continued over the years to press for off-road "single-track" routes. While the number and length of such trails remained somewhat limited, the District consulted regularly with the cycling community on trail-related decisions for both existing parks and new ones.

As the District's newer parks and trails took shape and matured, both road cyclists and mountain bikers of all ages and abilities could in time take advantage of a variety of routes, from flat paved regional trails to challenging remote backcountry trails. Of the District's 1,100 miles of trails, approximately 900 miles of unpaved trails—about 80 percent—have been designated as suitable for cycling (usually wider multiuse trails). Cyclists also enjoy 130 additional miles of paved regional trails.

By continuing to consult the Bicycle Trails Council of the East Bay—as well as the East Bay Area Trails Council for trail protection and advocacy—the District has worked to serve cyclists safely and well. The volunteer trail-safety patrol features a bicycle division served by knowledgeable and experienced cyclists who help promote safe and responsible riding.

Cyclists and hikers at Pleasanton Ridge in southern Alameda County

# Public Safety

Since its inception, the East Bay Regional Park District has set itself apart from other regional park agencies by managing its own comprehensive program of public safety. By providing police, fire, and other public safety services cooperatively with, but independently from, city and county agencies, the District's public safety division maintains the ability to meet the needs of sixty-five parks over a richly varied 1,750-square-mile area of responsibility throughout Alameda and Contra Costa Counties.

At peak summer season, the division employs some 500 people, including 125 full-time employees, half of whom are sworn police officers. The others include a range of safety specialists, from industrial firefighters to seasonal lifeguards. The Volunteer Trail Safety Patrol also serves in a public safety capacity, including some members who participate on the division's search and rescue (SAR) team. With 1,150 miles of trail to patrol, such volunteer service remains invaluable. Headquartered at Lake Chabot in Castro Valley, the division also maintains substations at the San Pablo Reservoir in Orinda, Contra Loma Regional Park in Antioch and, for air support, at the Hayward Municipal Airport.

"By land, by sea, and by air we provide around-the-clock services through a variety of specialized assignments," said Assistant General Manager Tim Anderson, who serves as chief of police, fire, and aquatic services. "Our safety services include the air support unit, the marine patrol, equestrian patrols, a K-9 unit, a special enforcement unit, an investigations unit, and a twenty-four-hour 9-1-1 communications center."

The public safety division also provides contract law enforcement services for recreational facilities in the Port of Oakland and for the East Bay Municipal Utility District (EBMUD) watershed and recreation facilities. By special agreement it fulfills policing needs on East Bay lands owned by the San Francisco Public Utilities Commission and at several state parks in the East Bay.

By undergoing a nationally recognized accreditation process through the Commission on Accreditation for Law Enforcement Agencies, the division maintains a commitment to meeting the highest standards of the public safety professions.

"Having been with the District for more than twenty-one years, I am very proud of our commitment to the community and the partnerships we have formed along the way," Anderson said. "Safety and quality of life are both personal and shared responsibilities. We strive to make our parks some of the nation's safest open space and recreation areas."

Police officers David Irvin (left, with his canine partner Baer) and Al Anaya (who retired in 2008): The mounted patrol unit provides important access within the East Bay regional parks.

in 1993, General Manager O'Brien could help establish a new level of training and inter-agency cooperation on wildland fire techniques, which differ substantially from those of the urban zone.

In 1994, four "remote automated weather stations" added to the District's growing mix of new technologies for preventing fire-related emergencies. Updated in 2001, the units continued to monitor weather and allow calculation of fire-danger indices, providing a complement to units operated by the City of Oakland and the state forestry department.

In 2009, after three years of staff and consultant effort, the District also created a comprehensive Wildfire Hazard Reduction and Resource Management Plan. The plan outlined a strategy for protecting lives and property through vegetation management of 3,600 hillside acres in thirteen regional parks, also coordinating with East Bay cities to provide neighborhood fire protection by educating homeowners and designing fire-safe homes and landscapes.

––––––––––––

Outside of wildland fires, two of the most challenging disasters to strike the District involved oil spills. The first occurred at Shell Marsh in the Carquinez Strait at the District's northern edge in April 1988, when the Shell Oil Refinery at Martinez spilled 432,000 gallons of San Joaquin crude oil into the marsh and the adjoining Peyton Slough. Filling the 100-acre marsh at the Martinez shoreline to a depth of more than four inches, the oil then flowed into the strait, spreading both upstream and downstream into Suisun and San Pablo bays.

The District owned no property near the spill site then, but as part of the mitigation from the State of California's $10 million Natural Resource Fund, it arranged in 1992 to purchase 200 acres of waterfront land and transform it into Waterbird Regional Preserve. The District collaborated with other governmental entities to create tide gates for cyclical exchange of saltwater and fish with the bay. With the "brackish" wetland thus restored, Shell Marsh was renamed McNabney Marsh in honor of the late Al McNabney, a stalwart of the Mount Diablo Audubon Society who helped establish the preserve and assure adequate public education and access.

The second oil spill—with far greater immediate effect on the District—began when the *Cosco Busan* container ship plowed into the Delta Tower of the Bay Bridge in a thick fog in November 2007, unleashing some 58,000 gallons of toxic bunker fuel into San

# Resource Enhancement Program

Since 1998, the East Bay Regional Park District's Resource Enhancement Program (REP) has worked to protect, restore, or mitigate the effects of human activity (or sometimes the effects of natural causes) on plant and animal habitats. By engaging in REP partnerships, the District has expanded the scope of many projects to meet multiple objectives, such as developing public access, preserving open space, linking protected areas to one another, or ensuring that development projects fully compensate for impacts on natural resources.

Although the District monitored and enhanced plant and animal habitats before the REP, outside entities often performed small, isolated restorations in developed areas, with little or no effort to account for affected species. Other entities purchased credits at mitigation banks far from the impact area. Now REP partnerships allow coordination of mitigation projects with regional goals and plans to achieve maximum benefits to natural communities and to nearby human residents.

REP projects have protected or restored tidal marsh, riparian wetlands, freshwater marsh, ponds, grassland, scrub, chaparral, and oak woodlands. Several special-status species have also benefited, including the Delta smelt, western burrowing owl, California clapper rail, salt marsh harvest mouse, San Joaquin kit fox, Alameda whipsnake, Diablo sunflower, and Alameda manzanita.

In the District's freshwater ponds and drainages, for example, the Amphibian Monitoring Project has long studied the threats to the California red-legged frog (a species listed as threatened by the U.S. Fish and Wildlife Service), the foothill yellow-legged frog (a federal and state "species of concern"), and the California tiger salamander (a federal candidate and state "species of concern"). By working closely with the U.S. Geological Survey and the U.S. Fish and Wildlife Service, District biologists identify and minimize the threats to these species—such as pathogens, contaminants, and nonnative predators—and coordinate responses to help protect, preserve, and recover these species.

Dozens of separate REP projects have protected or restored thousands of acres of public open space, including the plant and wildlife habitat, in these and other regional parks: Wildland vegetation enhancement projects have been coordinated in Brushy Peak Regional Preserve, Hayward Regional Shoreline, and Huckleberry Botanic Regional Preserve. Wildlife enhancement projects have been coordinated in Big Break Regional Shoreline, Black Diamond Mines Regional Preserve, Brushy Peak Regional Preserve, Diablo Foothills Regional Park, Eastshore State Park, Martinez Regional Shoreline, Martin Luther King Jr. Regional Shoreline, Morgan Territory Regional Preserve, Pleasanton Ridge Regional Park, and Vasco Caves Regional Preserve.

Francisco Bay. The spill affected thirty-one miles of shoreline under the District's protection in both Alameda and Contra Costa counties, as well as many miles of shoreline elsewhere around the bay. The District's disaster planning helped it respond quickly, working with the California Department of Fish and Game and other government entities, nonprofit organizations, and individuals to limit damage and to rescue birds and other wildlife.

Doug Bell, the District's wildlife program manager, releases a radio-tagged prairie falcon near Camp Ohlone.

Still, the damage took on astounding proportions, forcing closure of all or part of seven regional parks and requiring months of sustained cleanup and mitigation. Involved from the beginning in the District's response to the emergency, John Escobar, Assistant General Manager of Operations, later chaired an inter-agency committee formed to assess the spill response and apply its lessons to future efforts.

In addition to maintaining disaster prevention and response programs, the District's public safety division patrols the parks and enforces regulations under the leadership of Assistant General Manager Tim Anderson. The park operations staff, under Escobar, provides field presence throughout the jurisdiction and day-to-day management of all park resources.

Assistant General Manager Mike Anderson has shaped the evolving stewardship unit as part of the division of Planning, Design, Construction, and Stewardship. Wildlife biologists, botanists, and fisheries experts have long integrated natural resource management and other scientific stewardship techniques into the work of maintaining parkland ecosystems.

"Agencies oriented toward forestry have always been able to follow a clear path to appropriate stewardship," Anderson said. "But in a regional park district, with its orientation to interpretation and recreation vis-à-vis open space, the proper role of and methods for stewardship are not quite so obvious."

The District has steadily expanded scientific analysis to aid the protection of rare and endangered species, as well as common plant and animal life, and to facilitate wildfire hazard reduction, integrated pest management, and protection of important water resources at freshwater lakes, ponds, streams, and miles of bay and delta shoreline. The Resource Enhancement Program, established in 1998, has placed a strong emphasis on specific resource protection goals, such as maintaining species habitat and ensuring the integrity of natural wildlife corridors.

"The District is beginning to look at its resources in a different way," Anderson said. "We have learned that we need to take care of the land because it's changing on us."

Some regional parks have suffered infestations of yellow star thistle, cordgrass, and other invasive plants that threaten the natural ecosystem of the East Bay. The staff has faced infestations of invasive fauna as well, such as the freshwater mussels that hitch rides into lakes on trailered boats, bait buckets, and equipment. Once in, the mussels encrust hard surfaces, spreading to clog power plant and water intakes.

## Regional Parks Botanic Garden

Since its founding on New Year's Day of 1940, the Regional Parks Botanic Garden has represented a unique organization within the East Bay Regional Park District. Situated in Tilden Regional Park amid the dramatic natural beauty of Wildcat Canyon, the garden has become known worldwide as a primary research center for the collection, growth, display, and preservation of California native plants.

California's rich geography, nearly 160,000 square miles in all, features a range of distinct floral areas—seacoast bluffs, coastal mountains, interior valleys, arid foothills, alpine zones, and two kinds of desert. The wide range of vegetation native to these zones inspired the vision to organize the ten-acre botanic garden as "the state in sections," that can be walked in a single visit.

The collection includes nearly every California conifer and oak, a vast array of shrubs and perennials, and a comprehensive collection of California manzanitas, as well as significant collections of bunchgrasses, bulbs, and aquatic plants. Any plant specimen collected in the wild in one of the distinct natural areas must, according to the garden plan, reside in a corresponding part of the garden. The first annual blooms occur in early winter, providing a continuous show through the summer months by native plants with such fetching names as silktassel, mariposa, blue blossom, fritillary, bluff wallflower, fawn lily, and woolly blue curl.

In 1996, a group of volunteers founded the nonprofit Friends of the Regional Parks Botanic Garden to support the garden's educational, horticultural, and conservation efforts. Volunteers host an annual native plant sale in April and provide funding for improvement of paths, buildings, planting beds, and many other needs. Expert docents lead free garden tours on most weekends throughout the year.

In a rare continuity of leadership, Steve Edwards has served as director of the botanic garden since 1983, only the third individual ever to hold that post. Equipped with a doctorate in paleobotany from the University of California, Berkeley, Edwards also credits his garden elders, fellow staff mem-

View of part of the Botanic Garden in winter, with the seabluff in front of the juniper lodge, and the Sierran and Redwood sections beyond it

bers, and expert volunteers for his education. As a District employee since 1970, Edwards said, he became a "capable field botanist" under the tutelage of the masterful Walter Knight, also drawing direct inspiration and horticultural training from the garden's first two directors, James Roof and Wayne Roderick, and from Al Seneres, who was park supervisor under Roderick.

"A large number of plants growing in the garden are rare or endangered," Edwards said. "The collection serves as horticultural insurance for species threatened with extinction in the wild."

Fortunately, the botanic garden's staff and expert volunteers have set down their knowledge for a wider audience in these publications and a variety of professional journals:

- *The Four Seasons,* journal of the Regional Parks Botanic Garden
- *Manzanita,* newsletter of the Friends of the Regional Parks Botanic Garden
- *Guide to the Plant Species of the Regional Parks Botanic Garden* by James Roof, 1959
- *Guide to the Regional Parks Botanic Garden* by Walter Knight, 1983
- *Plants of the East Bay Parks* by Glenn Keator, 1994
- *Significant Plants and Animals of the East Bay Regional Park District* by Irja and Walter Knight, 1993

The restoration project at Alhambra Creek in Martinez in 2004, two years after its completion, included flood terraces and wetlands.

Five years after the restoration, Alhambra Creek's native wetland vegetation has filled in the previously barren areas and provides habitat for numerous native plants and animals, including the endangered California clapper rail and the salt marsh harvest mouse.

In addition to protecting and providing habitat for substantial numbers and types of wildlife, the District has for decades used carefully regulated and controlled grazing of domestic animals as a resource tool to help reduce fire hazards, encourage the natural cycles of native plants, and maintain the health of grasslands on which many species of wildlife rely.

Deer, elk, antelope, and other grazing animals made up part of the East Bay's ecosystem for thousands of years before settlement by nonnative peoples. Generations of Native Americans had used natural cycles to advantage, lighting fires to burn away stubble and then hunting the antelope, Tule elk, and other animals that came around to eat new grass that sprang up after the burns.

"When the Europeans first came here, they thought the Indians were pyromaniacs," O'Brien said, "but they were really doing land management."

Upon acquiring parklands whose recent history included grazing of domestic herds, the District began to integrate grazing into its grassland parks as a vegetation-management technique. Licensed and regulated under accepted principles of range management, grazing is used in approximately half of the sixty-five parks, mostly in spring and early summer, including some 5,000 cattle and 1,000 sheep. In 1983, the District pioneered the use of targeted "goat browsing" as a tool for fire prevention, and dozens of parks districts, public utilities, local governments, and researchers concerned with fire prevention followed suit with seasonal grazing of goat herds.

"Scientific research shows that if you manage grazing properly, it is a big benefit to the vegetation," O'Brien said. "Wildflowers, for example, grow tremendously if you manage grazing properly. If you don't, you have coyote brush and other highly flammable plants that eventually take over."

"In the Martinez fire of 2004, the District's grazing program probably saved several blocks of houses and the county hospital," Director Ted Radke said.

Overgrazing can be detrimental, too, inviting erosion and other vegetation-management problems.

"There was a time when we really didn't define grazing very well or understand it well ourselves," O'Brien said. The field staff knew the importance of grazing to fire prevention and to the land itself, but after sustaining heavy criticism for years the District set out to base its grazing methods more formally upon sound science.

Forming a grazing task force, the District began to study and refine its practices in collaboration with ranchers, fire departments, and environmentalists. Board members Ayn Wieskamp and Beverly Lane and Assistant General Manager Tom Mikkelsen (who preceded Anderson in managing the stewardship unit) led the effort to form working relationships with and prescriptions for grazing contractors as part of an ongoing education program intended to add to the knowledge of all parties.

"A lot of the land we obtained over the years came from ranching families, and they wanted to be able to continue grazing it," Wieskamp said. "While getting the benefit of that grazing, we wanted to make sure we were doing it properly and minimizing the effect on park users."

The Grasslands Monitoring Project, directed by a wildlife biologist and a rangeland ecologist at the University of California, Berkeley, began in 2002 to provide quantitative monitoring of the District's grassland properties. Through a growing body of annual research, the project helped the District assess its management of plant, bird, and small mammal communities in distinct vegetation sectors such as coastal prairie, riparian grassland, and—most extensive of all—valley grassland.

Research results indicated that environmental factors—rainfall, temperatures, soil chemistry, geographic features—rather than management activities caused most fluctuation in grassland plant and bird populations. "Regardless of the direction of the overall [environmental] trends however, where native plant species exist, native cover and species richness are generally higher in cattle grazed areas than in ungrazed areas," the researchers wrote.

"We've put a lot of science into this now," O'Brien said. "Our research completely changed U.S. Fish and Wildlife Service's approach [to managing valley grassland to benefit native species]. They were opposed to grazing, too, and after we gave them all the evidence and showed them how it was part of the ecology, they changed their position."

# Volunteers

From cataloging mining artifacts to providing safety patrols on remote trails, volunteers represent an important part of fulfilling the East Bay Regional Park District's educational and public safety missions.

"Our volunteers range from teens to retirees," said recreation services manager Anne Kassebaum. "The District has sixteen ongoing programs, so there's something for everyone, whether it's helping to remove invasive plants, assisting with trails maintenance projects, or monitoring owl boxes for the stewardship department."

Board member Ayn Wieskamp (Ward 5) has taken a strong interest in promoting volunteerism and expanding on the success of longstanding programs. "What impresses me is that this District has such a great number of volunteers," Wieskamp said.

According to Kassebaum, "In 2008 alone, nearly 12,000 ongoing volunteers provided the District with more than 120,000 hours of service. Here in the Bay Area, that service has a value of more than $2.4 million."

Director Beverly Lane (Ward 6) also has championed the cause of creating and maximizing opportunities for members of the public to donate their time and expertise to the District. "Volunteers bring a special energy to the District's parks," she said. "They introduce the public to parks, support the staff's work, and help keep our visitors safe."

The Volunteer Safety Patrol provides invaluable assistance throughout the East Bay Regional Park District by promoting safe and proper park and trail use by all park visitors.

Drawing upon her own background as professor of recreation, board member Carol Severin (Ward 3) worked with then-interpretive services manager Margaret Kelley to integrate volunteers into the interpretive program, where they now aid the staff in a variety of roles. Docents—volunteers who undergo specialized interpretive training—help promote in both kids and adults an appreciation of the plants, wildlife, history, culture, and ecology of the Bay Area by working alongside the naturalists, mainly at the District's visitor centers.

Since its inception in the 1980s, the Volunteer Trail Safety Patrol has grown into the largest of the volunteer programs. Under the auspices of the District's police department, volunteers in five patrol groups (mounted patrol, bicycle patrol, hiking patrol, companion dog patrol, and marine safety unit) assist professionals in (1) preserving the safety of park visitors and regional trail users, also educating them about resources, facilities, and programs, and (2) ensuring the safety of plant, animal, geological, historical, and archaeological resources.

Even the public affairs division reaps the benefit of volunteer ambassadors who represent the District to the public by providing information on hiking trails, park maps, interpretive and recreation programs, upcoming special events, and volunteer opportunities.

"This District was started by volunteers," said General Manager Pat O'Brien. "In all that time, since the 1930s, they have been one of our greatest assets."

In matters of public safety, disaster prevention, park operations, and resource management of flora, fauna, and land, the District has carefully refined its practices over many years, building a modern and comprehensive toolbox containing everything from grazing animals to helicopters.

The human element has proven to be the best tool of all for stewardship of the parks and the natural world. Within the District's own borders, no matter of human resources or expertise is left to chance. By hiring and retaining knowledgeable and dedicated employees to monitor land and wildlife throughout its two-county area, the District stands ready to act when opportunity arises or when disaster strikes.

As stewardship chief Mike Anderson said, "These folks are essential to our future."

Brushy Peak, a 1,833-acre regional preserve near Livermore, was acquired jointly by the Livermore Area Recreation & Park District and the East Bay Regional Park District. Brushy Peak supports a wide variety of wildlife species and a broad range of plant communities, of which California annual grassland is dominant.

## Chapter 9

# Strategy

*Everything about California is big, including its approach to financing land conservation.*

—MIKE McQUEEN and ED McMAHON,
*Land Conservation Financing*, 2003

As far back as the 1960s, the East Bay Regional Park District had made multiple attempts to annex the greater Livermore area, a 240-square-mile missing portion of its Alameda County territory. With the cities of Pleasanton and Dublin forming the western edge, and bordered by Contra Costa, San Joaquin, and Santa Clara counties to the north, east, and south, the region encompassed nearly a third of the county's 738 square miles. Murray Township, as the tract had been known since the nineteenth century, represented the heart of the Livermore Valley, but when Pleasanton voted in 1966 to join the District, the board of supervisors bowed to pressure from agricultural interests to exclude Murray Township from the ballot.

When Pat O'Brien became the District's general manager late in 1988, he knew he would revisit the matter of annexing Murray Township. Furthermore, he knew it could be done.

"The board had just written it off," he said. "They were convinced that they'd never be able to annex it."

In chairing the legislative committee of the California Association of Recreation & Park Districts over many years, O'Brien had long worked with committee member Bill Payne, general manager of the Livermore Area Recreation & Park District (LARPD).

Now he learned that LARPD had been a sort of barrier to the proposed annexation, in effect saying, "The East Bay Regional Park District can't come here, because we do regional parks."

While LARPD was, like the District, an independent "special district" of state government, it operated under a different section of the Public Resources Code. With a limited budget and a mandate to provide recreation facilities and sports programs in local urban parks, LARPD had nevertheless come under increasing public pressure to acquire and manage more open space, something it was not really equipped to do on a large scale after the budget cuts of Proposition 13.

O'Brien could, therefore, offer a solution.

He began talking with General Manager Payne about annexation, chatting up his old friend without a hint of pressure or confrontation.

"You must really want this badly," Payne ventured.

"No. I don't care, because I've got more than enough to handle," O'Brien replied. "But I think it's the right thing to do."

Payne had been pressured to cede partial jurisdiction over the years by O'Brien's predecessors, going back to the time of Dick Trudeau and even William Penn Mott.

"They were doing everything they could [to annex this area]," Payne said now.

But O'Brien seemed unconcerned, almost offhand. "Like I said, Bill, I just think it's the right thing to do for the people," he said. "But if it doesn't happen, that's okay with me."

Disarmed, Payne was at a loss. "Maybe we could work something out," he said cautiously.

"One more thing," O'Brien continued. "I can't do this without money. We've got to figure out some tax transfer."

Payne was incredulous. "You want money? Dick Trudeau never wanted money."

"Come on," O'Brien laughed. "You know Dick Trudeau is smarter than I am. Dick figured out how to do things all the time without money. I am not that smart."

Payne paused for a long moment. "You aren't as smart as Dick Trudeau, are you?" he said finally.

"No."

With that, an annexation was born. O'Brien put his assistant general manager for planning and design, Tom Mikkelsen, to work on it, also bringing parks expert Sy Greben from Southern California to consult.

Together the team worked out a unique cooperative agreement—later approved by the Local Agency Formation Commission—specifying that the two agencies would provide complementary park services and facilities for Murray Township, with a tax-transfer provision to be phased in over ten years.

Both agency boards supported the arrangement, and by 1992 the annexation had succeeded.

"It had to be somebody Payne trusted," O'Brien said later. "I think without the personal relationship, the conversation would never have happened."

With that milestone, the East Bay Regional Park District at last stood whole, serving as the regional park agency for all of Alameda and Contra Costa counties. Completing the two-county jurisdiction—annexations in Contra Costa in 1964 and 1981 and Alameda County in 1956, 1958, and 1992—had taken nearly sixty years.

---

In O'Brien's view, serving Murray Township and sharing its tax base was only one of several options available to diversify sources of outside funds for acquiring new parks and maintaining existing ones. Though he had devoted his entire career to park and recreation agencies, his financial orientation was not that of a government bureaucrat. As the board of directors was now finding out, he thought like a CEO.

As the new CEO for parks in the East Bay, he was discovering a number of fiscal areas where the board felt their options were limited. In some instances, they had been advised by outside professionals that some fund source or other was out of reach. O'Brien thought otherwise.

"Although the revenue was good, it was limited," he said. "They had never branched out in terms of looking at their overall portfolio and seeing how to create other sources of revenue."

To O'Brien, the focus on a broad and varied financial portfolio was, by now, second nature. Having been mentored at Southgate Recreation and Park District by big thinkers for whom "even the sky was no limit," he could scarcely conceive of being content with the status quo.

"Money was just a tool at Southgate," O'Brien said. "We always asked ourselves, 'How do you get more money? How do you increase your toolbox?' We were very pragmatic about it."

In reviewing the financial picture for the East Bay, O'Brien could not help thinking about how to increase the District's capacity for growth while making it more financially resilient.

One of his early innovations was to create an "assessment district" for a portion of eastern Contra Costa County that had been excluded when most of the county voted to annex to the District in 1964. Known as Liberty Union High School District, this section of east Contra Costa stood in the fertile San Joaquin delta zone that was, among other things, an agricultural center since 1903 for production of asparagus. Each year growers carefully shipped a seasonal harvest of slender green spears across the U.S. and as far away as Japan. The asparagus producers saw no need for a regional park agency that might encroach on their livelihood.

The District had, in 1981, seized an opportunity to annex this section of eastern Contra Costa, a good move even without an associated tax base. The property tax revolt known as Proposition 13 had been in effect only a short time then, and the public was in no mood to approve new taxes, however modest.

The assessment district—a revenue-generating mechanism to pay for specific services via property taxes—had become a major financial mechanism at Southgate after O'Brien, as general manager, led a push to change state law.

At that time, the early 1980s, assessment districts existed for exclusive use by cities and counties. Special districts were ineligible, with one little-known exception O'Brien happened to uncover while attending a conference on local government finance. A conference presenter, an attorney from Los Angeles, said special districts had to go through county authorities to create assessment districts. The only exception was the Landscape and Lighting Act of 1972, which was designed to support such projects as median strips in highways. It was, in fact, codified under the highways and bridges code, but it did give special districts the independent power to create assessment districts.

O'Brien returned to Sacramento and promptly read the Landscape and Lighting Act for himself. It clearly stated that eligible projects included trees, lighting, landscaping, lawns, and pathways, but not structures. That certainly sounded like a park, he thought. Southgate's attorney agreed.

Coordinating with a local developer who was poised to build one of many new residential areas east of Sacramento, Southgate conceived a plan to create new parks alongside the new homes. Potential buyers would see on their real estate disclosures a modest sum in property taxes that would go to parks each year. So far, so good.

O'Brien's legislative experience told him, however, that amending state law to expand both the scope of eligible projects and the debt-service provisions of the Landscape and Lighting Act was a matter for high-level players. He would bide his time.

Before long, he got the opening he sought when a parks colleague from Rancho Cucamonga contacted him in his role as legislative chair for the California Park & Recreation Society.

The passage of Measure KK in 1996 ensured a steady, dedicated revenue source for maintaining the East Bay Regional Park District's extensive trail system throughout Alameda and Contra Costa counties. Above, hikers enjoy Diablo Foothills Regional Park (Contra Costa County).

The Irvine Company, one of the largest developers in the state, had on tap a new residential development. Irvine wished to donate two parcels for parks, but no money existed to convert the land for recreational use, which would include such facilities as a sports complex. Was there some legislative thing that could help Rancho Cucamonga create these parks?

"There is something," O'Brien told him. "There's this Landscape and Lighting Act, but it needs some amendments to do all the things you need."

The executive director of the state Building Industry Association (BIA) didn't like the idea of amending the act. But the president of the Irvine Company got on the phone to him, along with the parks director and the BIA's lobbyist. When they all told him they wanted the amendments, he quickly agreed to comply.

If Southgate—a mere recreation and park agency—had tried on its own to amend the act for use by special districts, it would have been unlikely ever to succeed. But with the BIA out front, the legislation went right through, expanding the range of eligible park development options to include structures and also opening up a whole range of possibilities for repaying debt at a lower overall cost using notes and bonds.

# Ted Radke: Thirty Years of Service

Ted Radke can easily recall the particular day in 1964 when he first learned about the East Bay Regional Park District. While in training as a recreation director, he heard General Manager William Penn Mott's rousing speech about the campaign to annex Contra Costa County. The District then served portions of Alameda County alone, but its founders thirty years before had envisioned a regional park agency for both counties.

Born and raised in Richmond, Radke already had found in his working class parents a strong influence for his love of the outdoors. Named after his father (who was himself named for Theodore Roosevelt), Radke grew up learning to hike, camp, fish, and hunt while hearing stories about Roosevelt's and John Muir's adventures as early conservationists.

Radke was just eighteen when he heard Mott speak, and he convinced his parents to vote for the annexation. As his own environmental interests took shape, he got to know the likeminded district attorney and county counsel for Contra Costa, John Nejedly, who went on to the state senate, and Hulet Hornbeck, who soon became the District's first land acquisition chief.

While earning a master's degree from San Francisco State University, where he helped found the environmental organization Ecology Action, Radke traveled to three Midwest colleges as a featured speaker on the first Earth Day in April 1970. He moved with his wife, Kathy, to Martinez and began teaching political science at Contra Costa Community College, a career that continued for thirty-five years.

Radke greatly expanded his community service and environmental activism while still in his twenties. Elected to the Martinez City Council in 1972, he made an early mark by opposing development of the Martinez shoreline. He cofounded Contra Costa's branch of Ecology Action—where he had early input on the California Environmental Quality Act (CEQA)—and was active in the Association of Bay Area Governments.

He worked closely with his representative in the state assembly, John "Jack" T. Knox, the principal author of CEQA, and with his state senator, Nejedly, who chaired the Wildlife and Natural Resources Committee. When Paul Badger decided to vacate his seat on the East Bay Regional Park District board, he hoped Radke would replace him.

Elected to the board in 1978, Radke was reelected seven times and served for more than thirty years as the representative for Ward 7, which includes the cities of Brentwood, Antioch, Pittsburg, Martinez, Hercules, Pinole, Oakley, and Discovery Bay. Radke was instrumental in the acquisition of Martinez and Carquinez regional shorelines, Waterbird Regional Preserve, and Crockett Hills Regional

Park, as well as Vasco Caves, Big Break, Bay Point, and Clayton Ranch, and he helped the District increase the size of Briones Regional Park and Black Diamond Mines Regional Preserve. The District's total landholdings more than doubled during his service.

"The best way to save the environment is to buy it," he said.

Radke has chaired the board's legislative committee throughout his tenure, bringing his substantial knowledge, personal contacts, and effective lobbying skills to bear on the District's liaison with the legislative and executive branches of state government, as well as with the East Bay's delegation in the U.S. Congress. He has enjoyed a particularly productive collaboration over the years with Congressman George Miller, who supported all of his election campaigns and each of the District's ballot measures and other major initiatives.

Ted Radke, the longest serving member of the East Bay Regional Park District board of directors, was first elected in 1979.

As a board member, Radke advocated for creation and implementation of the Integrated Pest Management program begun by the District in the 1980s to require ecological management of parklands while reducing pesticide use. He was instrumental in setting the stage for—and pressing the full board to support—the District's first major capital bond, Measure AA, and the companion transportation measure in Contra Costa County, both of which won voter approval in November 1988.

"Our history includes three critical turning points," Radke said. "One was the founding of the District in 1934. The second was the annexation of Contra Costa County. That was 1964. The third was Measure AA."

As the sole board member still serving twenty years later, Radke helped design and carry out the successful renewal of AA, which went before voters as Measure WW in November 2008. "By passing Measure WW, voters recognized our past success at preserving open space," he said. "Looking ahead, our mission is still the same. Get money. Buy land."

"That's how I leveraged the Landscape and Lighting Act," O'Brien said later. "One, I found out I could use it, and, two, I amended it to allow all kinds of uses for park acquisition, development, and maintenance, as well as better financing."

Southgate took criticism at first from people in the profession.

"You're double taxing," some cried. "It's not fair. You can only spend the money in the area you've got the assessment district. What about other areas that don't have it?"

In time, though, many special districts used Landscape and Lighting themselves and found it worked well to finance selected park and recreation needs.

Now managing East Bay parks, O'Brien faced another challenge. When he floated the idea of an assessment district to the board of directors, they assured him the District had already studied the matter. They had brought in a top firm to consult and were advised that an assessment district was not practical or achievable.

"That's funny," O'Brien said to himself. "I've done six of them."

After convincing his own bosses that they could and should support the concept, O'Brien moved in 1991 to create a Landscape and Lighting Act assessment district in east Contra Costa County, which was the focus of much of the District's activity for new parks.

"We were buying parks like Round Valley," he said. "We were doing a lot more projects out there, but we needed revenue to help support that."

Again, O'Brien assigned his planning manager, Mikkelsen, to collaborate with consultant Sy Greben. They selected prominent community members for an East County Task Force that would advise on recommendations to the board. The District also, in 1993, created a second Landscape and Lighting assessment district to fund crucial maintenance for the growing network of trails throughout both counties, which park users had named a top priority.

But within a few years, board member Ted Radke learned the Landscape and Lighting Act itself might change dramatically. If statewide Proposition 218, "Voter Approval for Local Government Taxes," passed in the 1996 general election, assessment districts would be subject to a majority vote of affected property owners—not all voters—rather than the current system of public notification without a vote. The District would no longer hold independent power to create or renew assessment districts.

"This proposition essentially precluded benefit assessment districts as we knew them," Radke said. "We would lose the ones we already had."

For the only and final time, Radke suggested, the board could decide to go to all voters—not just affected property owners—in the same 1996 general election to seek support of existing assessments before the law changed. If they waited, and if Proposition 218 passed, they would face not only the task of winning property-owner support for assessments labeled as brand-new property taxes, but also a list of other new barriers in the law.

With little lead time, the District crafted and qualified two measures for the November 1996 ballot. Measure LL would renew the assessment district for park operations in eastern Contra Costa, a critical need in the absence of a tax base. Measure KK would renew trail maintenance for both counties, a significant aspect of overall park operations that typically attracts attention only when it fails. With approximately 1,000 miles of trails within the regional parks and another 150 miles linking trails to each other and to the communities they served, maintenance provided direct service to hikers, cyclists, and equestrians alike. It also played a key role in public safety, especially fire prevention.

"Without these funds, we're not going to have trails that are as safe and attractive as they are now," said Director Beverly Lane. "It's essential that we go ahead with this."

Each measure required a simple majority to pass, and voters polled before the election appeared satisfied with their park agency and ready to continue the existing relationships. Both measures did pass by more than two-thirds, and Proposition 218 passed statewide as well. Again, the board and staff's strategic assessment of options and careful preparation for an election had achieved a milestone for regional parks.

While the District engaged in this series of bold steps to improve the total financial picture, it simultaneously faced an economic recession that was changing the picture for property taxes, which still provided some 80 percent of operating funds.

"The state budget crises started coming like waves," O'Brien recalled.

Invoking its power to "shift" money from local government entities to the Education Revenue Augmentation Fund (ERAF), the state created a formula that would transfer $3.6 billion in permanent property tax revenue for 1992–1993 from counties, cities, and special districts to schools, reducing its general fund obligation to schools by the same amount.

Upon hearing this, O'Brien huddled with the District's lobbyist, Bob Houston, to strategize about how to protect the District from the economic devastation of the proposed shift. By zeroing in upon the differences between single- and multicounty special districts—a distinction that had been codified in the aftermath of Proposition 13—they devised an alternative formula that would protect the few multicounty agencies from the ERAF shift. Now they had to convince the legislature.

Assembly members Johan Klehs and Tom Bates lent office space and staff to Houston to aid the District's preparation for the state budget showdown. When the appropriate moment arrived, O'Brien made a beeline for Sacramento. As budget negotiations dragged on, reaching fever pitch in the wee hours, the change to the ERAF formula was off, then on, then off again. Assembly Speaker Willie Brown had given his word that no exceptions would be granted. But when a handful of members, led

In 1982, then-General Manager Dick Trudeau hired Ternes and Houston (now the Houston Group) to represent the East Bay Regional Park District's interests before the California legislature and in key state agencies. Bob Houston (right) has represented the District since that time. More recently Doug Houston (left) has taken a lead role in representing both the District and the California Park & Recreation Society.

by Delaine Eastin, marched into his office and threatened to hold up the whole budget over the formula, he relented.

"That was a horrendous battle," O'Brien recalled. "Three times in one night we lost $14 million out of our budget—which would have been a permanent tax shift—and at the end we saved it."

"I remember driving back as the sun was rising, and I just couldn't believe it," he added. "We were the only agency that pulled off anything like that."

More than a decade later, in the throes of California's budget process, the state finance department again proposed augmenting the ERAF as a mechanism for fiscal relief, constructing another formula to shift local government agency funds to education.

"That would have devastated us," O'Brien said. "It would have taken about $34 million out of our property tax."

In a deal brokered with Governor Arnold Schwarzenegger, a formula had been accepted by cities, counties, and even the California Special Districts Association. Many large special districts—water districts and the like—had taxing power based upon rates charged to provide services. Under the proposed formula, "nonenterprise" agencies like the East Bay Regional Park District whose budgets were based instead on property taxes would take a far greater hit to their budgets.

"This is totally unacceptable," O'Brien told the board. "We're not going to let it happen."

O'Brien consulted with Doug Houston, who had taken over much of the lobbying business from his father, Bob Houston, in Sacramento. Together they devised an alternative formula specifying that "enterprise" (rate-based) districts, which could generate revenue, would bear an appropriate share of the burden.

With no other agencies willing to act, the District rallied alone, going directly to East Bay legislators to make a case that the tax "shift" favored rate-based agencies. The governor would get what he wanted—no argument there—but the way he proposed to get it, at least on the special district side of things, was unfair.

With Doug Houston's leadership, the East Bay's legislative delegation agreed to take up the fight to change the formula in Sacramento. As a result of their efforts, especially those of Senator Tom Torlakson, the cuts to nonenterprise special district budgets were not nearly as deep as everyone had feared.

"We saved all the recreation and park districts throughout the state this way, too," O'Brien said. "They would have been crippled."

The District's savvy campaign garnered recognition later on, even a few thank-you calls, but at the time no other special districts would join the battle. Fearful that tinkering with the formula might make them worse off, they accepted their fate. The District was on its own to study the state's plan and then propose and defend a change.

None of it, however, would have succeeded without the ability to draw upon a long-standing alliance and sense of common purpose with the legislators, whom O'Brien called "our board in Sacramento."

"The strength of our relationship with our legislative delegation is the way we were able to defeat that earlier formula," he said.

The immediate result for the District of this second round of property tax "shifts" was a budget cut of just $9 million. After facing a possible cut of $34 million, the outcome could hardly have been better.

---

The economic woes of the early 1990s brought still another result in the form of lowered property assessments, which gradually decreased operating revenue from property taxes just when El Nino storms caused enormous parkland damage. Unforeseen mitigation and rebuilding costs gobbled up operating funds, threatening the public's usual level and quality of access to all parks in the growing system.

Although maintenance might have seemed an insignificant or secondary matter to the casual observer, the District's board and staff saw every day the effect that operations and maintenance had on the experience of every park user. As the direct interface with the public, the field staff took seriously the obligation to maintain these lands for present and future generations, both for their enjoyment and for their safety.

"Land doesn't protect itself," the late park supervisor Roger Epperson told the *San Francisco Chronicle* in 1998. "The first step is acquisition, to save it from development. The second is a perpetual commitment to quality maintenance and upkeep."

Just as passage of Measure KK in 1996 assured top-quality and sustained operations and maintenance for trails throughout the District, the board put forth Measure W to serve the same function in the parks themselves.

# Thirty Years of Proposition 13

Proposition 13, the statewide property tax revolt passed by voters in June 1978, represented a massive change in public financing for California. By severely limiting property tax increases, it cut the associated funding to all local and regional public agencies, including such basic city and county services as schools, libraries, and parks.

Before the election, then-General Manager Dick Trudeau invited coauthor Howard Jarvis to present the Jarvis-Gann initiative at the California Park & Recreation Society's annual conference in Fresno. He also invited opponent Peter Behr, who represented Marin County in the state senate and had tried already to pass a softer brand of property tax cuts.

Jarvis arrived inebriated, Trudeau reported later, and divulged to attendees that his intent in drawing up Proposition 13 on his dining room table one weekend was to slash state tax levies, not to cripple local public agencies.

"He didn't know what he was doing," Trudeau said. "It hurt the state less than it hurt the local governments."

Although the District had to forfeit 50 percent of its tax base—revenue that would have funded operations as well as land acquisition and new park development—Trudeau led a restructuring of District finances and forged ahead with ambitious plans for growth.

As public policy, Proposition 13 and its effects prompted a whole genre of study within and beyond California. By the measure's thirtieth anniversary in 2008, a large body of research existed on the legislature's failure to head off the ballot-box showdown in the first place and on the myriad changes to public financing that followed.

One such shift that carried over indirectly but strongly to the District was the "fiscalization of land use," in which cash-strapped cities and counties openly evaluated land-development proposals based upon their potential to generate revenue rather than their value to the community.

Proposition 13 also spawned several derivative ballot measures. In 1986, voters passed Proposition 62, a statutory initiative requiring majority voter approval of local general taxes and two-thirds voter approval of local special taxes. California court decisions later allowed cities, counties, and local governments to impose new general taxes or increase existing ones—such as user taxes and business license fees—without voter approval.

Proposition 218, "Voter Approval for Local Government Taxes," went before voters in the November 1996 election. Principally sponsored by the Howard Jarvis Taxpayers Association, it was passed by 56.5 percent of voters statewide.

"The Jarvis/Gann forces were playing for keeps," wrote public policy analyst Revan Tranter in *Governing California,* "insisting not only on (a) retroactivity, but (b) reversal of laws and traditions, to place all burdens of proof on the local agencies, and (c)—most tellingly—the ability to reduce or repeal through the initiative process any local tax, assessment, fee, or charge."

Alerted to Proposition 218 before the election by longtime board member Ted Radke, the District pulled off a skillful preemptory strike. By going voluntarily before voters in the very same election, the board and General Manager Pat O'Brien preserved two "assessment districts" they had created under the Landscape and Lighting Act to provide critical funding of park operations. The hard lessons of Proposition 13 had not been forgotten.

Below are some selected sources on Proposition 13:

- *A Digest Summarizing California Voter Opinions About Proposition 13 Thirty Years After Its Passage,* written and published by the Field Institute, 2008
- *After the Tax Revolt: California's Proposition 13 Turns 30,* edited by Jack Citrin and Isaac Martin and published by Berkeley Public Policy Press, 2009
- *Governing California: Politics, Government, and Public Policy in the Golden State,* edited by Gerald C. Lubenow and Bruce E. Cain and published by the Institute of Governmental Studies Press, 1997
- *Patterns in California Government Revenues Since Proposition 13,* written by Michael A. Shires and published by the Public Policy Institute of California, 1999
- *Proposition 13: 30 Years Later,* written and published by the Public Policy Institute of California, 2008
- *Surviving Proposition 13: Fiscal Crisis in California Counties* written by Valerie Raymond and published by the Institute of Governmental Studies Press, 1988

Placed on the ballot in November 1998, a time of economic upswing, the measure hit a snag early on when two retired board members, Harlan Kessel and Mary Jefferds, along with representatives of several environmental groups, came out in public opposition.

In all, ten people signed the official ballot argument against (or the rebuttal to the argument for) Measure W, focusing not on the measure's subject matter but on a particular District personnel matter with which they disagreed, the discipline of a former employee-union leader who had been promoted into management in human resources.

Huckleberry Botanic Regional Preserve was one of the parks to benefit from improved environmental maintenance after voters passed Measure CC in November 2004.

"Don't reward heavy-handed personnel tactics with an open checkbook," advised the ballot-pamphlet argument against Measure W.

Signers in favor included board president Jean Siri, Nobel laureate Glenn Seaborg, and retired state senators John Nejedly and Nicholas Petris.

Although the measure won 64.7 percent of votes, it fell less than 2 percent short of achieving the two-thirds majority needed for passage. Clearly, opponents had swayed voters. The District would have to retreat and regroup.

In the primary election of March 2002, the board again put forth a parcel tax for voters to decide. Four critical needs would be addressed if Measure K succeeded: environmental maintenance, fire prevention, public access, and resource protection and restoration.

This time the measure enjoyed formal support from key environmental groups—the Sierra Club, two chapters of the Audubon Society, and Save the Bay—including several that had remained neutral the first time around.

Again the measure garnered a majority of yes votes, 65 percent in Alameda County and 57 percent in Contra Costa, but again it failed to achieve the necessary two-thirds. Though it had polled strongly ahead of time, it may have suffered from a sagging economy and the poor turnout of the early March primary.

After the second defeat, O'Brien and the board sought a different approach. Taking a hard look at the distribution of votes for the failed Measure K, they saw that it had been most strongly supported in the populous western area—the District's oldest section—from Oakland to Richmond.

"I asked myself a simple question," O'Brien recalled. "Where is it passing? Those are the voters who want the measure. Let them vote for it."

After a careful study of options by their longtime pollster, George Manross, they drew up a third parcel-tax measure that would fund critical operations and environmental maintenance in the twenty-one regional parks of that western area, including the original parks established in the 1930s. To the board's credit—and to their relief—this last effort passed as Measure CC in November 2004.

With that success, the District's financial portfolio for operations achieved an equilibrium of sorts, ensuring that future growth would be matched by responsible stewardship. In the process, the board and their CEO had become a sophisticated and dynamic financial team. Their work together, however, would soon take on added urgency. Available open space for new parklands was fast being depleted, while the primary mechanism for buying land, the Measure AA bond funds approved by voters in 1988, would soon run out.

Valley floor in springtime, Round Valley Regional Preserve in Contra Costa County

## Chapter 10

# Arrival

*The conservation movement has matured, withstood the backlash of monied interests, and with climate change threats, is poised to become a truly global effort. But even as we "think globally" we must "act locally." We must be as far sighted as the thousand East Bay residents who got together in 1931, during the Great Depression, to form the East Bay Regional Park District.*

—SETH ADAMS, Director of Land Programs,
Save Mount Diablo, 2008

Due east of Mount Diablo, on some of the least developed open space remaining in Contra Costa County—indeed, in all of California—rancher Jim Murphy grew increasingly worried. For some years, he had tried to imagine what would become of his spread, Round Valley, after he passed on. In the mid-1980s, already approaching age eighty, he suffered something of a shock when Contra Costa County supervisors zeroed in on his land as one of five possible sites for solid waste landfill. In the plain language Murphy preferred, they needed a garbage dump.

By 1986, the controversial search for suitable land had escalated into the "dump wars," with Save Mount Diablo and other organizations working to prevent the county from invoking its power of eminent domain to condemn a site. By then, however, Murphy had come to a decision of sorts. He would never allow his 700-acre home, purchased in 1873 by his Irish immigrant grandfather and maintained as a family ranching and farming operation ever since, to become a trash heap.

Murphy had, over the years, earned a reputation as an eccentric throwback to an earlier time. Trespassers on his land would, likely as not, be chased off with a rifle and an inelegant phrase or two. Now, however, a representative was on the way from the

# Habitat Conservation Plan for East Contra Costa County

In 2007, the East Bay Regional Park District joined Contra Costa County and a group of cities, agencies, developers, landowners, and conservation groups to implement the East Contra Costa County Habitat Conservation Plan, the largest such plan in Northern California. A joint-powers authority created to coordinate regional conservation within a 175,000-acre area of Eastern Contra Costa County, the plan earmarked some 30,000 acres of critical wildlife habitat for preservation over the next thirty years.

Since the 1980s habitat conservation plans (HCPs) have been a successful tool to incorporate regional habitat protection into growth planning. By satisfying the federal Endangered Species Act and streamlining the endangered species permit process of the U.S. Fish and Wildlife Service and the California Department of Fish and Game, HCPs represent an important planning mechanism allowing environmental interests, landowners, and developers to plan efficiently for growth alongside local governments. All parties agree beforehand on zones for development, habitat conservation, and mitigation fees.

"It's a win-win for everyone," said board member Ted Radke. "Residents get more open space and recreation opportunities, wildlife habitat is preserved, regulatory obstacles are streamlined for businesses and developers, rural landowners have an expanded market should they wish to sell, and local governments have more control over crucial infrastructure projects."

With no other agencies offering similar capabilities, the District made a substantial long-range investment as an implementing agency for the East Contra Costa County HCP. The District took on the role of acquiring and operating individual habitat conservation projects, while pursuing additional funding to assist those operations. Development fees and government grants and bonds would fund implementation costs—estimated at $350 million—including land purchases, land management, and site improvements.

Board members Radke (Ward 7) and Beverly Lane (Ward 6) served on the HCP executive governing committee, along with ten other city and county representatives. A large coordination group, including Contra Costa County's principal representative, John Kopchik, District representatives Brad Olson and Beth Stone, and many others, helped develop the final HCP. The District's land acquisition chief, Bob Doyle, worked to make the land purchases a reality.

"In the first two years we had seven different projects under way," Radke said. "The program has been enormously successful."

East Bay Regional Park District. This man had called first and would not be a trespasser, but Murphy would greet him in full uniform—cowboy hat, boots, rifle. He intended to find out just what this park fellow was made of.

As the District's new assistant general manager for land acquisition, Bob Doyle had laid careful plans for this meeting, working closely with Save Mount Diablo to master the political situation before making the appointment with Murphy. As a Concord native, he knew the area well, and he drove south on Marsh Creek Road with a sense of purpose.

As Doyle pulled up to the ranch house and got out, Murphy paused a moment before speaking, cradling the rifle sideways across his chest.

"What do you think of mountain lions?" the rancher asked.

Doyle felt a wave of doubt pass over him. Was this some sort of trick question? Would the wrong answer be a deal-breaker? He, too, paused.

"What do you think?" he shot back.

Murphy leaned back and smiled. "I kind of like them," he said.

Doyle let out his breath. The land business never ceased to surprise him. In just a few seconds, the old rancher had shattered the stereotype of the cantankerous, gun-toting foe and had offered a patch of common ground. The two men still had a few details to work out—more than a few—but over the next couple of months Doyle and the board of directors cobbled together $40,000 for a two-year option to buy Round Valley.

"Some of the landowners are challenging people, but they're good people," Doyle said later. "It's about finding out who they are face-to-face."

Just when the 1988 bond, Measure AA, promised to revitalize the District's ability to buy land, Murphy relinquished his ranch at a bargain price, just under $1.4 million, in keeping with his wish that it be preserved as open space. Parcels purchased later from his family expanded Round Valley Regional Preserve to 2,000 acres of grassland, oak woodland, and riparian habitat, all of which opened to public use in 1998, the year after Murphy's death.

"That valley shows you what east Contra Costa County looked like," said the District's general manager, Pat O'Brien. "Development never happened there, so it's actually preserved."

An abundant home for wildlife, including nesting golden eagles, a threatened species of red-legged frog, and the endangered San Joaquin kit fox, the preserve also forms the southern end of a wildlife corridor rising northwest along Marsh Creek and all the way to the Carquinez Strait.

In spite of the political tension surrounding the acquisition of Round Valley, O'Brien didn't fault the Contra Costa board of supervisors for considering the site, but he was relieved that the District was in a position to protect such a rare, pristine landscape from their intervention.

"These aren't bad folks," he said. "They have a responsibility to find appropriate landfill. Their interests just conflict with our interests."

"There's a big difference between having a regional park district that's independent and having a county park department," he added, "because you're last in the pecking order if you're the county park department. The county can say a dump's got a higher priority than you do, and that's it."

———————————

As with Round Valley—a dozen years in the making—land acquisitions often took years to complete, and opening of actual parks could take much longer. As William Penn Mott had long ago stated, it was necessary to think ahead twenty-five years when it came to parks.

One acquisition that took at least that long to mature was Camp Arroyo, a residential camp for kids located in the southernmost part of inland Alameda County. The process had begun in the early 1970s when the District purchased land near Camp Parks, a U.S. Army installation east of Dublin. Intended as a regional park called Tassajara, the property had a revisionary clause stipulating that, should a military crisis or other urgent need arise, the federal government could take it back. When the first Gulf War flared up, the military made noises about using Tassajara for medical evacuation training. Meanwhile, Alameda County was seeking a suitable site to build a BART station in Dublin, where the federal landholdings included a promising site.

The county owned but had no immediate use for the remote Camp Arroyo property, which had served for many years as a sanitarium for patients with tuberculosis. After the sanitarium closed, leaving the grounds in disrepair, the county leased it out as a home for wayward kids. That operation had taken an additional toll on the buildings and the land itself.

With Dave Collins, the assistant general manager of management services, serving as liaison with the military, the District studied the situation and proposed an unusual solution. If all parties agreed, Representative Fortney "Pete" Stark would sponsor legislation in Congress to facilitate a three-way trade.

The District would give up Tassajara and in return would acquire the county's former tuberculosis property. No money would change hands, but the county would have to tear down some buildings and clean up the site so that the District could use it. The county would get other federal property for the BART station.

Taking the long view, the District also negotiated a revisionary clause on Tassajara. The property would become part of Camp Parks, but if ever the army's need for it expired—always a possibility in the future—the land would revert to the District. Such a turn of events would make the whole arrangement a sort of "two for one" for parks.

Upon acquiring the property, the District wasn't quite sure at first how to put it to best use. O'Brien had hoped one day to provide a camping facility for kids, but he knew that adding something like that to an existing park might invite opposition from those who considered such activities outside the District's purview or who worried about the effects on the land. Perhaps the site of a former tuberculosis sanitarium wouldn't arouse too many objections.

Like all facilities at Camp Arroyo, the dining hall was constructed with "green" building techniques. It is the largest building in the U.S. using rice bales as insulation.

Also, during the state budget crisis of the early nineties, O'Brien had noticed some legislators beginning to question his agency's relevance.

"A legislator from Southern California told me, 'You're one of the reasons we have a budget crisis—too much government.'" O'Brien said. "There were a lot of people in Sacramento not interested in helping us at all."

O'Brien began to think the District had to have more reason to exist than preserving open space. In recent years it had moved gradually from a park orientation to an environmental orientation. Some board members, he felt, would have gone completely to open space if they could.

"I was saying you've got to have both," O'Brien recalled. "You have to have a social function, not just a natural function. We also have to invest in kids."

"Everybody says this is the environmental generation," he added. "I say, maybe not. What are kids really doing? Watch behavior, not language. Behavior says this is the least environmental generation we have ever had. It's the video generation. Their parents don't even want them to go outside. What value are kids really going to have for these properties when they grow up if they don't have experience of them?"

As O'Brien saw it, the District needed to communicate to constituents that it had an important reason to exist, not superior to preserving open space, but separate and distinct from it. One way to involve children with the natural world was to create a residential environmental education camp.

"We've got to do this," he told the board. "We have to have social relevance."

The Camp Arroyo site was damaged goods, he told them. Creating a camp would not harm wildlife. If anything it would, over time, reintroduce and nurture flora and fauna. The budget situation would, of course, make it difficult to move forward. But what was crisis if not opportunity?

In a serendipitous turn of events, The Taylor Family Foundation contacted the District to ask if anyone knew of ten acres they could buy to build a summer camp for kids with life-threatening illnesses. Noting the similarities of intent, the District conceived a plan to share the Camp Arroyo site. During the regular school year the District would provide weeklong environmental education camps for urban kids. The Taylor Family Foundation would move its existing summer program to Camp Arroyo, offering it to seriously ill kids without charge. With that agreement in place, The Taylor Family Foundation raised $3 million to help build the facility, continuing to raise additional funds each year.

By careful planning and pinpoint timing, the District funded the creation of Camp Arroyo on an even grander scale. With bipartisan support in the legislature, O'Brien and the board seized upon the "dot-com boom" that swelled state coffers in the late 1990s, winning $6.5 million in budget augmentations from Sacramento over two years. Under Rosemary Cameron's direction, the Regional Parks Foundation raised separate funds to furnish the new camp and then took over the campership program itself, continuing to pull in some $120,000 each year to send kids to camp.

Camp Arroyo's curriculum, designed to meet state standards, exposed participants to environmental education concepts such as sustainability—directly informed by the natural world and by the "green" architecture of camp facilities—while also ensuring they would have fun. That, after all, was what camp was all about. Like kids everywhere, these campers would look back one day and realize their experience had stayed with them all of their lives.

While the success at Camp Arroyo grew out of unique circumstances, the District took other steps to renew its earlier emphasis on increasing public access to all parks. The board, in its policy-setting role, agreed on the importance of providing programs to attract a wide variety of users. One result, some years in the making, represented a leap forward in public service but also a significant change to the internal culture.

The concept of environmental education had appeared in the District's original 1934 charter, and as the District's primary educational liaison with the community, the interpretive services department had been a particular priority of every general manager since the 1960s. Interpretive programs were the main public attraction at Ardenwood Historic Farm, Black Diamond Mines, and Coyote Hills.

In offering interpretive programs for schoolchildren starting in the 1970s, individual naturalists enjoyed great freedom to design their own programs. This flexibility stood in sharp contrast to the practices at some agencies, whose chief naturalists might assign both the topics and the content of programs.

"Our interpreters . . . were given an unusual amount of time to plan and prepare programs . . . and to become intimately familiar with what they were going to teach," the former chief naturalist, Ron Russo, recalled. "We had a limit on the number of students per program . . . ideally, it was twenty or less."

The District had always offered many programs that could be considered "recreation"—swim lessons, organized hikes, and fishing and kayak lessons—but they were offered in different departments or led by naturalists and never referred to as recreation. The very notion of recreation met with resistance by some who viewed it as outside the agency's mission.

Naturalist Linda Yemoto engages her young audience and their parents at Tilden Regional Park's Environmental Education Center. Naturalists offer a wide variety of hands-on environmental education programs for all ages.

Over time, General Manager O'Brien worked with the board to evaluate programs and construct an organizational solution that would enhance access to all public programs. By creating a recreation services unit in 1994 as an equal counterpart to interpretive services, the District consolidated dozens of recreational offerings while greatly expanding the number of patrons who could participate. Russo now oversaw both interpretive and recreation services, and when he retired—after thirty-seven years of service—Rick Parmer succeeded him as chief.

Elected to the board in 1994 after fourteen years on the board of the Hayward Area Recreation and Park District, Carol Severin brought expertise as professor of recreation at San Francisco State University. She, too, had found resistance in some park settings to the concept of recreation—sometimes termed the "R-word"—but O'Brien and her new colleagues supported her efforts to promote programs for a variety of users.

An instructor teaches youngsters how to bait a fishhook in a recreation program at Crab Cove.

"Recreation programs are the hook that gets families into the regional parks and introduces children to interests of a lifetime," she said.

Beyond the matter of offering organized programs, the larger issue of public access remained at the forefront. As with all public space, the growing network of regional parks drew individual and group users with special recreational and environmental interests. On trails, hikers and birders had to coexist with cyclists, equestrians, and trail runners, while at the lakes and beaches, swimmers might meet people in canoes and kayaks or on fishing boats or sailboards. This rich variety of users, the board felt, represented a fundamental part of the District's mission. A high priority on providing parks suitable for many uses, they knew, also meant that park management had to be well thought out and carefully executed, with public safety foremost.

Within the staff ranks, operating procedures grew somewhat more formal during the 1990s so that no part of the District's work would become too entrenched. Prompted to review priorities regularly, the staff could implement service changes where necessary to respond to Bay Area's growing population. The board often restated one core value, lest the staff slip into complacency and forget: The District exists to provide the finest possible regional parks and services to current constituents and future generations. Land acquisition is a top priority, especially as the total amount of open space continues to shrink. While buying land, however, the staff must stay in touch with the needs, views, and preferences of the taxpayers who finance and use the parks.

This challenge from the board led the staff to seek out cutting-edge business practices to expand their knowledge of and responsiveness to park users. Having made extensive use of surveys and polls since putting Measure AA before the voters in 1988, the District came to embrace these techniques for measuring and responding to other things.

A periodic series of user surveys in regional parks and on trails, also conducted by behavioral scientist and pollster George Manross, began to yield important data about how users think about parks and what they want from their park experiences.

In an early 2008 survey, for example, 96 percent or more of respondents agreed with separate statements that the regional park system (1) was a valuable public resource; (2) improved their quality of life; and (3) must be properly maintained for present and future generations to enjoy. While the survey went on to measure user satisfaction, it also asked about the District's level of responsibility, accountability, and trustworthiness. These questions aimed to quantify something quite apart from mere satisfaction, something that had never before been articulated.

"We borrowed from the corporate world [the distinction between] satisfaction and loyalty," General Manager O'Brien said. "Public agencies usually just settle for satisfaction."

"Satisfaction is not a motivator for action." he added. "Loyalty is 'satisfaction plus' and being willing . . . to take action."

Building upon this concept, the District adapted sophisticated communication methods from the private sector with the goal of transforming users' natural loyalty to their local parks into a stronger identification and loyalty to the regional parks "brand" throughout the East Bay. Citizens aware of and loyal to the regional park system would more likely take positive action, whether volunteering to help build trails or voting in favor of a bond measure. If loyalty existed, people might more readily voice their needs and specify how well those needs were being met.

The District also began to review and improve its formal planning process. The master plan adopted in 1973 had undergone multiple revisions, including one that was nearly complete when O'Brien arrived as general manager in 1988.

"It basically envisioned continued expansion . . . and identified properties and park enhancements throughout the park district," he said. "There was also a vision to have more parks in east Contra Costa County, because we had annexed it in 1981 and really didn't have appreciable parks to show for it yet."

While it was a good blueprint that allowed the District to accomplish many things, O'Brien thought the next master plan might do well to increase strategic planning while ensuring an efficient process to accomplish goals.

Lifeguards provide swim instruction to youngsters at Roberts Pool in Roberts Regional Recreation Area in Oakland.

The East Bay Regional Park District's strong emphasis on public safety includes maintaining a helicopter, shown here by Officer Doug Jackley at a safety fair.

"I think in 1997 we improved the plan, made it a little more focused," he said. "It was much more of a public process ... whereas I think the revision prior to that was much more of an insular process."

A key tenet of the 1997 master plan, a simple ten-word phrase growing out of that public input process, served to carry the District into the twenty-first century with a clear sense of priorities articulated and shared by constituents. The board, the staff, and the Park Advisory Committee united behind this message, simply stated yet carrying a great weight: "An environmental ethic guides us in all that we do."

———————————

As the twenty-first century approached, the District's priorities and overall direction reflected a gradual but dramatic transformation of its board of directors. Ted Radke, Jean Siri, Doug Siden, Beverly Lane, and Carol Severin had each been reelected at least once. With the addition of John Sutter in Ward 2 and Ayn Wieskamp in Ward 5, the board became an ever more collaborative team, working together to solve increasingly complex issues. Sutter, a retired judge of the Alameda Superior Court who also had served as Oakland's vice mayor, also brought to the board substantial experience with the Association of Bay Area Governments, the Bay Conservation and Development Commission, and Greenbelt Alliance. Wieskamp, a veteran of local government, had served on the Livermore City Council, the Livermore Area Recreation & Park District board, and the Alameda County recycling board.

After Wieskamp's election in 1998, the board enjoyed a stable membership for nearly eight years. Gone were the days of taking sides to eke out a bare majority in the boardroom. These members approached their work as colleagues and collaborators, each using the power of elected office to advocate for constituents.

Already a twenty-year veteran, Radke alone was in a position to compare. "We all had the same general goals, and everybody was very civil," he said.

Jean Siri of Ward 1, first elected in 1992, experienced something of a transformation herself. With rock solid credentials as an environmentalist and as mayor and council member of El Cerrito, she arrived ready to make changes. After initially voicing the views of a few naysayers, she soon developed a sophisticated grasp of how the District operated and why and, in so doing, became highly collaborative and effective.

"She became a terrific board member," Radke recalled.

While running for her fourth term in 2004, Siri was asked if she had thought of retiring so that younger candidates might serve.

"Only if I have a dead body would I stop running," came her spirited reply, "and it's not quite dead yet."

In 2006, while still serving on the board after a dozen exemplary years, Siri succumbed to a heart attack at the age of eighty-five. True to her word, she had not stopped running voluntarily.

Siri's sudden death set off a contest among those who thought of succeeding her. Although an election for Siri's seat in Ward 1 was still two years off, the board opened up the position so interested individuals could apply for appointment to the seat until the 2008 election. Fourteen people responded.

The board considered several strong contenders, including Shirley Dean, a former mayor of Berkeley; Whitney Dotson, a member of the Park Advisory Committee; and Norman La Force, an active member of the Sierra Club whom the board also knew from the East Bay's environmental forum.

After several months, however, the directors selected Nancy Skinner of Berkeley as their new colleague for Ward 1. Skinner had served on the Berkeley City Council for eight years, leading a caucus at the national League of Cities to prevent federal preemption of ozone-depletion regulations in the Clean Air Act.

A former member of Alameda County's training and employment board and recycling board, she had local government expertise in both energy efficiency and environmental protection, and she had been active in the creation of Eastshore State Park.

"She elevated the park district's concept and use of green technology," O'Brien said. "She was able to move that part of the agenda up very well."

As it turned out, Skinner was destined for bigger things. After just two years, she was approached by local Democratic leaders about running for the state assembly. Owing to term limits, the incumbent, former Berkeley mayor Loni Hancock, would run for the state senate in November 2008. Both she and her husband, Tom Bates—who had switched elective offices with her and was now Berkeley's mayor—wanted Skinner to run.

Skinner hesitated. Having found a happy niche at the District, she had only just begun to produce the solid accomplishments she envisioned. In time, however, the Democratic powers convinced her she had the ability and credentials to become an effective state legislator.

# Board of Directors

**WARD 1  Whitney Dotson, elected 2008**

A retired public health administrator for Contra Costa Health Services, Dotson served on the District's Park Advisory Committee from 2006 to 2008 before being elected to its regular board. He brought a long history of community and environmental advocacy in Richmond, where he played a key role in the long process of annexing Breuner Marsh to Point Pinole. He also served on the board of Citizens for Eastshore State Park.

**WARD 2  John Sutter, elected 1996**

A former vice mayor and council member of Oakland, Sutter was also a deputy district attorney for Alameda County and a judge of the Alameda County Superior Court. He helped to found People for Open Space (now Greenbelt Alliance) and served as its president for seven years, working since the 1960s to end filling of the bay and to provide public waterfront access at what is now Martin Luther King Jr. Regional Shoreline. He has served on the boards of the Association of Bay Area Governments, the Bay Conservation and Development Commission, the Sierra Club, the San Francisco Bay Restoration Authority, and the YMCA.

**WARD 3  Carol Severin, elected 1994**

Before joining the District, Severin served fourteen years on the board of the Hayward Area Recreation and Park District. Now retired from the recreation faculty at San Francisco State University, she was instrumental in expanding the District's intern program, which places college students from a variety of academic departments in the greater Bay Area. She also served on the boards of California Association of Recreation & Park Districts, the California Special Districts Association, and the California Park & Recreation Society. In 2000, she received the prestigious Pugsley Award, one of the highest honors in the field of parks and recreation.

**WARD 4  Doug Siden, elected 1992**

The former executive director of an environmental education and recreation program for the American Baptist Churches, Siden also has served on the board of the Martin Luther King Jr. Freedom Center at the Martin Luther King Jr. Regional Shoreline within his ward (where he aided a San Francisco Bay Trail extension and new park facilities). He chaired the District's election campaigns for Measure K (2002), Measure CC (2004), and the major bond extension, Measure WW (2008). He also has championed conversion of the former Alameda Naval Air Station to public use and the completion of the San Francisco Bay Trail.

### WARD 5  Ayn Wieskamp, elected 1998

Before serving at the District, Wieskamp was a member of the Livermore City Council for eighteen years. She also served on the boards of the Livermore Area Recreation & Park District and the Alameda County Recycling Board. A former public school teacher, she continues to teach recreation classes. She cochaired the District's grazing task force, and in 2008 she became the special district representative to Alameda County's Local Agency Formation Commission (LAFCO).

### WARD 6  Beverly Lane, elected 1994

A former mayor of Danville, Lane was the founding president of the Danville Association and the Museum of the San Ramon Valley. She was president of the Eugene O'Neill Foundation, Tao House, and California Elected Women's Association for Education and Research and served on the League of California Cities State Board. She helped initiate the Iron Horse Regional and Calaveras Ridge trails and the Contra Costa Transportation Commission. A cochair of the District's grazing task force, she advocates for effective volunteer programs, trail expansions, and care for the District's cultural resources.

### WARD 7  Ted Radke, elected 1978

In addition to teaching political science at Contra Costa Community College for thirty-five years, Radke served on the Martinez City Council, cofounded Contra Costa Ecology Action and Eco-Information, and played an active role with the Association of Bay Area Governments. A strong advocate for all District bond measures, notably AA (1988) and WW (2008), he also chaired the board's legislative committee for more than thirty years and championed the Integrated Pest Management Program and the Habitat Conservation Plan for East Contra Costa County.

The 14th assembly district, encompassing the westernmost parts of both Alameda and Contra Costa counties, had for years remained so heavily Democratic that any nominee of that party was sure to win in a general election. The entire contest was in the primary, when candidates would vie for the Democratic nomination.

Skinner ran an effective campaign, helped in part by studying the District's polls and making a conscious decision to associate her name with the regional parks. Featuring

The Quarry Lakes Regional Recreation Area in Fremont (Alameda County), thirty years in the making, includes what is believed to be the largest freshwater lake in the U.S. located entirely within a city. Mission Peak Regional Preserve is visible in the distance.

park photographs in her campaign materials, she touted energy efficiency as essential to the environment outside the voter's door. She handily won the Democratic primary in June 2008 and, unopposed in the general election, she became the first board member to win a seat in the legislature.

"People have a big loyalty to the park district brand," O'Brien said. "The fact that she ran based upon many of those concepts and won the seat shows the strength of that message."

The board and staff knew Skinner would do well in Sacramento. The fact that the District had been her stepping stone elevated their own work, they felt, and brought a certain recognition to their park agency. It was, and had always been, a place of leaders, a key player in local government and in the parks field. As the largest regional park district in the nation, both in acres and in population served, it had started out in the vanguard of regional park agencies and stayed there.

The November election would now include a local race to replace Skinner in Ward 1. To no one's surprise, both Norman La Force and Whitney Dotson filed as candidates. Both men had strong environmental and local government credentials, and both were well known in their communities. Both candidates had been board members of Citizens for Eastshore State Park and had urged cleanup of contaminated sites at the Richmond shoreline and opposed the building of casinos there.

But La Force, an attorney who had served as mayor and council member for El Cerrito, was the powerhouse of the two. As chair of the San Francisco Bay Chapter of the Sierra Club, he had more political experience and many local endorsements, including the Sierra Club, supervisors from both counties, and the mayors of Richmond, El Cerrito, Albany, Berkeley, and Emeryville. Dotson, though favored in the Contra Costa County portion of Ward 1, was embarking on his first election. A retired public health program director, he was serving on the Park Advisory Committee while continuing his lifelong community advocacy in Richmond.

But voters delivered a surprise at the ballot box. Though La Force garnered more votes in Alameda County, Dotson drew enough support in both counties combined to put himself over the top, pulling off an upset.

O'Brien, though taking no role in the election, was as surprised as anyone.

"Whitney didn't seem to have the horsepower that Norman did. It was interesting to see how it all unfolded," he said. "Usually, if you've got the Berkeley vote, that overwhelms Richmond, but not this time."

---

Throughout 2008 the contest in Ward 1, fascinating though it was, took a distant second place in the minds of all District board and staff members. Two years before, the board's seven directors had begun to review the agency's history and conduct a serious evaluation of its future. Nearly seventy-five years had passed since the East Bay Regional Park District's founding in 1934 as a "special district" of state government, and a full thirty years had elapsed since California voters had approved the sweeping property tax revolt known as Proposition 13, which changed forever the funding picture for local government agencies, including special districts.

At the thirtieth anniversary of Proposition 13, the board could take pride that the District had compensated effectively for the steep drop in property tax revenue that had threatened to sink all local government entities. The passage of Measure AA in 1988 had helped preserve 34,000 acres of open space (exceeding by 25 percent the goal of 27,500 acres), while creating seventeen new regional parks, adding more than 100 miles of trails, and funding $60 million in neighborhood recreation projects—rehabilitating a senior center in Richmond, building baseball fields in Pleasanton, constructing a portion of the Delta de Anza Trail in Pittsburg, and everything in between—a total of 235 separate grants. In all, the District had nearly doubled the $225 million investment of its citizens, leveraging money to secure matching funds at no cost to local taxpayers. The bond measure was a success by any measure, made possible by a visionary board willing to take on difficult new acquisitions and by the staff's strategic management of fiscal and operational aspects.

Now, however, came a dilemma. The District's major mechanism for financing land acquisition, direct and matching funds from Measure AA, would soon run its course.

In the late 1990s, Director Radke had learned that nearby cities were refinancing existing bonds at lower interest rates. He suggested the District do the same for Measure

AA debt. That move alone, carried out by finance chief Dave Collins, had saved $14 million. Nevertheless, all bond funding was fully committed.

The twenty-first century was well under way, and relatively little open space remained available in the District's two counties. The land program still teemed with activity, but in two more decades, three at most, all open space would be spoken for. The acquisition game would be over for good. With Measure AA funds nearly exhausted and fully committed, what form should the District's next twenty years take? It made sense to continue bond funding for land acquisition while open space remained, but how and when should voters be asked to consider it?

By starting early with polling and other proven research tools, the board soon agreed in principle on a clear path of action. Unless something happened to call them off course, they decided, they would, in the general election of 2008, ask voters to approve a bond, not a new one but an extension to the existing one with no increase in the existing property tax rates.

"It was important to make it an extension and not increase the tax rate," Radke said.

After careful polling to determine voters' financial thresholds, the board settled on a bond measure of $500 million.

"That figure took our breath away," said Director Doug Siden, "but we knew we could back it up with a solid financial plan tied to specific land acquisitions."

Having played in the major leagues of land deals for years, the board knew this was the next logical step in the District's mandate to convert open space to parks. Furthermore, they were confident that voters would support it.

Of the $500 million, $375 million (75 percent) would fund regional park acquisitions and capital projects, while the other $125 million (25 percent) of the proceeds would—as before—go to cities, special park and recreation districts, and county service areas for their park and recreation services. Indeed, owing to a sagging economy and a troubled financial picture for California itself, most future local and regional park projects would depend on funding from an extension of the bond. Only the greater Livermore area, known as Murray Township, would be excluded from the election, as it had joined the District after the passage of Measure AA. The new measure, carefully designed as an extension of an existing tax, could not include a tax that was new to one area.

The board's approval process, while not simple, proved considerably smoother and less conflicted than the process of 1988. Using the "go-no go" model their pollster followed—just like a NASA space mission—they continued to evaluate the measure's prospects. By early summer, with the deadline looming to file for inclusion on the ballot, they had their answer. The $500 million bond extension was a go. On July 1, 2008, the board voted 7–0 to place the measure on the ballot. Coming precisely twenty years after Measure AA, the bond extension would again benefit from the high turnout of a presidential election year.

After general deliberations, polling, and scrutiny of every item on the proposed project list, the board could now oversee the process of crafting ballot measure language while continuing voter research and carrying out a public information campaign. As the summer drew to a close, the seven directors—with Director Siden chairing the campaign—worked their individual wards to raise awareness and encourage support for the bond extension.

Sycamore Valley Regional Open Space Preserve near Dublin, with a view toward suburban Danville. Acquisition of Sycamore Valley helped establish regional open space as a recognized category of East Bay parkland.

Having weathered the frantic run-up to Measure AA twenty years before, Radke found the current challenge a pleasure by comparison.

"We could point to the success of Measure AA and to projects in each community funded by AA," he said. "We had credibility."

The first sign of trouble came when the Contra Costa County registrar of voters determined that the formal ballot title of the bond measure—"Extend Existing East Bay Regional Park District Bond at No Increase in Tax Rate"—would count as part of the seventy-five-word maximum allowed to describe the measure. Not only was this a different method than the District had seen before, it was different from Contra Costa's own method for the recent Measure CC in 2004.

Alameda County—the measure's "lead county" owing to its larger population—disagreed with Contra Costa's interpretation, saying the seventy-five-word maximum did not include the title. But the Contra Costa registrar refused to back down. With no time to go to court, the District recast the measure to seventy-five words, including the title.

# Regional Open Space, Wildlife, Shoreline, and Parks Bond Measures

|  | Measure AA | Measure WW (extension of AA) |
|---|---|---|
| Date of election | November 8, 1988 | November 4, 2008 |
| Amount of capital bond | $225 million | $500 million |
| Property tax rate (per $100,000 assessed value) | 10 cents | 10 cents |
| **Voter approval rates** | | |
| Percent required to pass (two counties combined) | 66.7 percent | 66.7 percent |
| Alameda County result | 69.8 percent | 72 percent |
| Contra Costa County result | 64.9 percent | 71.4 percent |
| Total two-county result | 67.6 percent | 71.7 percent |
| **East Bay Regional Park District share** | | |
| Land acquisition | $126.6 million | $281.3 million |
| Park development and rehabilitation | $ 42.2 million | $93.7 million |
| Total | $168.8 million | $375 million |
|  | (75 percent of bond) | (75 percent of bond) |
| **Local park and recreation agency share** | | |
| Grants program | $56.3 million | $125 million |
|  | (25 percent of bond) | (25 percent of bond) |
| **Results (Measure AA only)** | | |
| Open space and shoreline acquired | 34,000 acres | |
| Miles of trails added | 100 | |
| Number of local grants | 235 | |

With a sigh of relief, the campaign committee returned to preparing the ballot argument "for" and the rebuttal to the argument "against" Measure WW, as it was now titled. Jerry Kent, retired from a forty-one-year career at the District and now volunteering on the campaign, happened to visit the Alameda registrar's office to pick up papers in advance of the filing deadline.

"I'll submit the arguments to you by next week," he told the clerk.

"Oh, no," came the reply. "We need them today."

"Today?" Kent couldn't believe it. "Your web site said next week."

"Oh, the web site was wrong, and we had to change it. The due date is today."

The Alameda registrar had changed the deadline, and there was no choice but to comply. The argument language had been drafted, of course, but Kent had only hours to complete the paperwork, chase down multiple signatures, and submit the package before five o'clock closing. Surely, he thought, nothing else could go wrong.

When absentee ballots had been mailed and voting had begun, the staff and the campaign committee breathed sighs of relief. It was a Friday in October, and O'Brien even thought of leaving a couple of hours early. They had done all they could. Now they had to stand back and let the voters decide.

Just then, Ted Radosevich, the agency's attorney, walked in.

"I hate to break this to you," he said, "but Alameda County didn't print the titles of any local measures on the absentee ballots."

O'Brien stared at the ballot. Measure WW consisted of the boxed ballot statement with no title. Beside the box were the words "Bond Yes" and "Bond No"—not simply "Yes" and "No" as usual—a change appearing on some local measures but not others. The missing title—with its essential phrase "at no increase in tax rate"—was the worse problem. O'Brien and Radosevich went to see the registrar that very day. Their complaint was duly noted and another meeting arranged for the next business day, Monday, to convey a response. On Monday the registrar, saying the law was vague, announced that ballots would not be reprinted to add local measure titles for the District or anyone else.

Campaign mailer developed by the "Yes for Parks" campaign with the aid of two consulting firms (Barnes, Mosher, Whitehurst, Lauter & Partners; and The Next Generation) helped to promote voter support for Measure WW, EBRPD's $500 million bond measure approved by voters in November 2008.

The East Bay Regional Park District's board of directors and general manager in 2009: Back row from left are board member Whitney Dotson, Vice President Doug Siden, board member Ayn Wieskamp, President Ted Radke, General Manager Pat O'Brien. Front row from left are Secretary Carol Severin, board member John Sutter, and Treasurer Beverly Lane.

Before they were out the door, O'Brien turned to Radosevich. "We're suing these people right now," he said.

Consulting an expert election attorney, they learned that the county had violated the elections code. The registrar's only legal authority to change the title was to abbreviate it "if necessary." The law granted no authority to eliminate it completely.

All ballots for Alameda County had been printed, and both absentee and early in-person voting had begun. The District filed suit, and immediately the county counsel relented. In settlement discussions the county claimed the ballots could not be reprinted in time. The printer disagreed but, afraid of holding up a presidential election, the registrar offered instead to send a letter to every registered voter explaining the error and providing the correct title. The District accepted, and 800,000 letters went out while the staff unleashed a hastily conceived flash flood of public information. Now, once and for all, the election rested in the voters' hands.

On November 4, 2008, as Americans went to the polls to elect Senator Barack Obama of Illinois to the White House, voters in the California counties of Alameda and Contra Costa also cast ballots on Measure WW, which would affect their quality of life for years to come. By election day, the District operated sixty-five regional parks on nearly 100,000 acres, also overseeing 1,100 miles of trails and serving more than 2.4 million residents in the two counties. The District now asked voters to expand on the success of Measure AA by approving a $500 million extension without an increase in property tax rates.

As the District prepared to celebrate its 75th anniversary in 2009, voters came through, passing Measure WW at an approval rate topping 71 percent, far exceeding the two-thirds majority required for passage. An exit poll analysis showed a loss of four to six percentage points traceable to Alameda County's ballot error, but voters there, as usual, approved the measure at a higher rate than voters in Contra Costa County. This time Contra Costa's "yes" votes had increased, and the two were almost even.

This result acknowledged, as nothing else could, twenty years of exceptional leadership and park stewardship by the District's board of directors and staff since passage of the 1988 measure. Even more important, the election confirmed seventy-five years of vision by ordinary citizens, whose strong connection to their open space had never wavered since they gathered one thousand strong at the Hotel Oakland in 1931 and then overcame every challenge to create the East Bay Regional Park District in 1934.

In such a dynamic, complex, and densely populated community as the East Bay, people's lives grew richer if they had ample opportunities to seek solitude or come together in the exquisite setting afforded by California's geography, climate, and natural resources. Over the next seventy-five years—perhaps more than ever—the people of the East Bay would need, and they would have, a living landscape whose full possibilities had yet to be revealed.

East Bay Regional Park District managers and staff: From left are Mary Mattingly, administrative support manager; Bob Doyle, assistant general manager, Land Division; Cinde Rubaloff, chief financial officer/controller; Mike Anderson, assistant general manager, Planning, Stewardship, and Development; Susan Gonzales, human resources manager; Rosemary Cameron, assistant general manager, Public Affairs; Ted Radosevich, District counsel; Allen Pulido, clerk of the board; Dave Collins, assistant general manager, Finance and Management Services; Tim Anderson, assistant general manager, Public Safety; John Escobar, assistant general manager, Operations; and Pat O'Brien, general manager.

The oak and bay woodlands of the Ohlone Regional Wilderness shelter endangered bald eagles, mountain lions, bobcats, deer, and a herd of tule elk. Seen here from Mission Peak at afternoon's golden hour, the Ohlone is open to hikers and equestrians via the Ohlone Wilderness Trail, which passes through several regional parks.

# Epilogue

On January 13, 2009, the board of directors of the East Bay Regional Park District conducted its first meeting of the new year. Elected on the same day as President Barack Obama in November 2008, Whitney Dotson now took his oath of office as the people's elected representative for Ward 1, which encompassed a string of cities on the eastern edge of San Francisco Bay, taking in portions of both Contra Costa and Alameda counties.

Dotson joined a board—Directors Ted Radke, Doug Siden, Beverly Lane, Carol Severin, John Sutter, and Ayn Wieskamp—that had repeatedly extended its reach, combining a certain moral courage with a well-oiled process to lead the District to unprecedented accomplishment and financial stability. With sixty-five regional parks, more than 1,100 miles of regional trails, and 14 million park visitors each year, this board set policy for the largest regional park agency in the nation.

In the two months since the election, the board and the staff of 650 also had basked in voter approval of a different sort. In passing the all-important bond extension, Measure WW, at more than 71 percent, constituents of both counties had voiced clear support of the District's methods and results of the past twenty years since the original bond, Measure AA, passed in 1988. Now authorized to proceed at the significant level of $500 million in general-obligation bonds for new and expanding capital projects, the agency could begin the new year with a clear mandate.

The timing could hardly have been better, as 2009 marked the official seventy-fifth anniversary of the District's founding by forward-thinking citizens of 1934, who taxed themselves at the height of the Great Depression to create parks. Three-quarters of a century later, a sizable list of new projects, compiled and carefully refined over two years, would now go forward with Measure WW funds, including $8 million toward restoring urban creeks, $16 million to create a new park at the former Concord Naval Weapons Station, more than $65 million for trail projects in both counties, and more than $13 million to acquire parkland on Pleasanton Ridge. These and more than fifty other clearly defined and budgeted projects would take shape with the District's full measure of technical expertise, political acumen, and financial discipline.

While offering the public a year of participatory events in the parks in celebration of the seventy-fifth anniversary, the District grappled with the economic turmoil that caused the State of California to reduce funding to all special districts and other local governments. Carefully preserving jobs, the District implemented budget cuts elsewhere and, owing to carefully planned and managed financial resources, remained in better economic shape than many comparable agencies.

The anniversary year proved the right time to embark on another major project, revision of the 1997 master plan. Already equipped with a recent update of the map of existing and potential properties—prepared in advance of the vote on Measure WW—the District now began the long process of scrutinizing the guiding policies of the plan itself. It would likely take another two years to complete this work, as the essential participation of thousands of citizens, dozens of stakeholder groups, and local governments still lay ahead.

The board and staff already had begun to articulate some of the principles they knew would appear in the next master plan, such as working from an environmental justice framework or considering the effects of global warming on land, water, and people.

"The time has come to make explicit some of the concepts we already use in our work," said Mike Anderson, Assistant General Manager for Planning, Design, Stewardship, and Construction.

The District would move ahead with this, as with all things, with a remarkable focus. As agents of taxpaying citizens, the board and staff would think big, acting from a position of legal and ideological strength, in order to manage the land placed under their protection and provide an excellent system of parks and trails.

In a fitting bit of symmetry, the seventy-fifth anniversary in 2009 included another watershed event. In late October the land title to 1,156 additional acres of Pleasanton Ridge transferred from private hands to the East Bay Regional Park District. Purchased with partial funding from Measure WW, the acquisition also won financing from the Altamont Landfill Open Space Committee and from an ongoing partnership with the Priem Family Foundation.

"This is the District's single largest land acquisition since 1990," said land acquisition manager Nancy Wenninger.

With few large open space parcels still in play, this property at Pleasanton Ridge represented a significant purchase in a ridgeland area that had suffered intense controversy and, ultimately, unprecedented collaboration for twenty-five years. With the new parcel, a total of nearly 6,500 acres of Pleasanton Ridge had been saved.

"As with many of the District's important projects, it took years of effort by many individuals and organizations to make it happen," Wenninger said.

With the purchase of the 1,156-acre Tyler Ranch property (viewed here from Foothill Boulevard in Sunol), located adjacent to Pleasanton Ridge Regional Park, the District surpassed the 100,000-acre milestone. The property extends for almost 3.5 miles along Sunol Ridge and includes steep, heavily vegetated slopes, open grasslands, and rock outcrops on the ridgetops.

 With the new acreage putting it "over the top," the District had, within seventy-five years of its founding, safely and irrevocably preserved more than 100,000 acres throughout the two counties.

 That extraordinary number, more than any other, would breathe life and a sense of purpose into the next seventy-five years. While the District applied bold leadership to new challenges, citizens of every race, color, creed, interest, or ability could embrace the regional parks of the East Bay, secure in the knowledge that 100,000 acres would remain, always, theirs to keep.

Vasco Caves Regional Preserve features spectacular rock outcrops set against the foothills of Mount Diablo. Its Indian rock art is evidence of human use nearly 10,000 years ago. Acquired jointly with the Contra Costa Water District, the preserve shelters endangered red-legged frogs, tiger salamanders, and fairy shrimp, and it provides habitat for kit foxes, eagles, and nesting raptors. Owing to the fragile resources, all public access is by guided tour.

# Appendix 1

## East Bay Regional Park District Leaders

**Board of Directors**

Charles Lee Tilden (1939–1950)

Leroy Goodrich (1939–1963)

August Vollmer (1939–1940)

Thomas J. "Tommy" Roberts (1939–1958)

Aurelia Henry Reinhardt (1939–1945)

Emery Stone (1940–1949)

John A. MacDonald (Ward 4, 1945–1972)

Robert Sibley (1948–1958)

Milton Godfrey (1950–1954)

John A. Mulvany (1954–1962)

Robert Gordon Sproul (1958–1967)

Clyde Woolridge (Ward 2, 1958–1976)

George C. Roeding Jr. (Ward 5, 1962–1970)

Marlin Haley (Ward 3, 1963–1974)

Mary Helen Calfee (1964)

John S. Bryant (1964)

Paul J. Badger (Ward 7, 1965–1978)

Fred C. Blumberg (Ward 6, 1965–1977)

James H. Corley (1967)

Paul E. Harberts (Ward 1, 1968–1972)

Howard L. Cogswell (Ward 5, 1971–1982)

Mary Lee Jefferds (Ward 1, 1972–1991)

John J. Leavitt (Ward 4, 1972–1988)

William F. Jardin (Ward 3, 1974–1982)

Harlan Kessel (Ward 2, 1976–1992)

Walter H. Costa (Ward 6, 1977–1986)

Ted Radke (Ward 7, 1979–present)

Donald G. Holtgrieve (1982)

(Mr.) Lynn Bowers (Ward 5, 1983–1987)

John O'Donnell (Ward 3, 1983–1994)

Kathryn Petersen (Ward 6, 1987–1990)

Jocelyn Combs (Ward 5, 1987–1998)

James H. Duncan (Ward 4, 1989–1992)

Carroll Williams (Ward 1, 1991–1992)

Oliver Holmes (Ward 6, 1991–1994)

Jean Siri (Ward 1, 1992–2006)

Susan Smartt (Ward 2, 1993–1996)

Douglas L. Siden (Ward 4, 1992–present)

Beverly Lane (Ward 6, 1994–present)

Carol M. Severin (Ward 3, 1994–present)

John H. Sutter (Ward 2, 1996–present)

Ayn Wieskamp (Ward 5, 1998–present)

Nancy Skinner (Ward 1, 2006–2008)

Whitney Dotson (Ward 1, 2008–present)

**General Managers**

Elbert M. Vail (1934–1942)

Harold L. Curtiss (1942–1945)

Richard Walpole (1945–1960)

Wesley Adams (1960–1962)

William Penn Mott Jr. (1962–1967)

Irwin Luckman (1967–1968)

Richard C. Trudeau (1968–1985)

David Pesonen (1985–1988)

Pat O'Brien (1988–present)

# Appendix 2

## Timeline

**1866**   Soon after the Civil War, Frederick Law Olmsted Sr., designer of New York City's Central Park, envisions "scenic lanes" in the East Bay hills. More than sixty years later, his sons will use it as the foundation of their proposal for a sizable East Bay park.

**1860s to 1920s**   Many small private water companies emerge to supply the growing East Bay. Canyons are dammed to create Temescal, San Leandro, Chabot, and San Pablo reservoirs. Small companies consolidate into the East Bay Water Company.

**1916**   The National Park Service is established, with Stephen T. Mather as its first director.

**1923**   A severe drought causes the public to demand a reliable water delivery system. The East Bay Municipal Utility District is created to pipe water from the Mokelumne River. After completing the project in 1928, the water district has more than 10,000 surplus acres of watershed land. Robert Sibley and Samuel C. May lead a grassroots movement to save and preserve this valuable open space.

**1928**   Voters approve a $6 million California State Park Bonds Act to establish the state parks system.

**1930**   The Olmsted Brothers (architects and sons of Frederick Law Olmsted) and Ansel F. Hall of the National Park Service write the Olmsted-Hall Report, "Proposed Park Reservations for East Bay Cities," making a compelling case for creating a 10,000-acre East Bay park.

**1931**   A thousand East Bay residents meet at the Hotel Oakland to advocate for the project outlined in the Olmsted-Hall Report. They petition the water company to create parks with its surplus watershed land, but the petition is refused. Mount Diablo (Contra Costa County) is designated a unit of the new state park system.

**1933**   The semiofficial Regional Park Board is formed, chaired by Elbert Vail of Oakland (who will in 1934 become the District's first general manager), to advocate for creation of the first regional park "special district" in the nation. California Governor James Rolph signs AB 1114, authorizing the new district, into law.

**1934**   A petition drive collects 14,000 signatures in support of an East Bay Regional Park District. The resulting ballot initiative passes on November 6 with 71 percent of the vote. The new agency will serve the cities of Alameda, Albany, Berkeley, Emeryville, Oakland, Piedmont, and San Leandro, governed by an elected board of directors: Major Charles Lee Tilden, Leroy Goodrich, August Vollmer, Thomas J. "Tommy" Roberts, and Dr. Aurelia Henry Reinhardt.

**1936**   The District opens the first three parks in October with a grand public celebration: Wildcat Canyon (renamed Tilden Regional Park after Major Charles Lee Tilden), Roundtop (renamed Sibley Volcanic Regional Preserve after Robert Sibley), and Lake Temescal. The 1936 budget totals $194,835. Works Progress Administration (WPA) laborers help build the parks.

**1937**   Tilden Golf Course opens, and the first regional golf championship is held.

**1939**   Redwood Regional Park is acquired: 1,494 acres for $246,277.

**1941**   The Brazil Building opens to the public in Tilden Regional Park. Originally part of the Brazilian pavilion at the 1939 World's Fair on Treasure Island, it was donated by the Brazilian government, and WPA crews constructed the stone exterior.

**1942**   After Pearl Harbor and the U.S. entry into World War II, 500 acres of Tilden Regional Park are turned over to the U.S. Army Defense Command for training. Harold L. Curtiss of the U.S. Forest Service becomes general manager. The staff of six (reduced from thirty) must manage 4,100 acres of public land.

**1945**   The war's end brings an era of prudent growth. Richard Walpole, manager of the golf course in Tilden Regional Park, becomes the general manager.

**1948**   The District acquires a vintage 1911 Herschell-Spillman carousel for Tilden Regional Park (owned and operated for many years by concessionaire Harry Perry). It is later listed in the National Register of Historic Places.

**1952**   Grass Valley Regional Park (renamed Anthony Chabot Regional Park after the engineer who built the Temescal and Lake Chabot dams) opens to the public.

**1953** Roberts Regional Recreation Area, 88 acres acquired in 1951 next to Redwood Regional Park and named for board member Tommy Roberts, opens to the public.

**1954** At the District's twentieth anniversary, the budget of $652,000 supports 5,400 acres of parkland, forty-seven full-time employees, forty-three seasonal and part-time employees, and an estimated 2.7 million visitors annually.

**1955** The Little Farm is built at the Tilden Nature Area with funds donated by the Berkeley Kiwanis Club. A major trail in Tilden Park is renamed Nimitz Way after Fleet Admiral Chester W. Nimitz at the suggestion of board president Robert Sibley.

**1958** Citizens for Regional Recreation and Parks, later to be renamed People for Open Space (in 1969) and then Greenbelt Alliance (1987), is organized by Dorothy Erskine and Jack Kent.

**1960** Save the Bay is established (as Save San Francisco Bay Association) by Esther Gulick, Kay Kerr, and Sylvia McLaughlin. Wesley Adams becomes the interim general manager.

**1961** The District is licensed to create and operate regional recreation areas at Don Castro and Cull Canyon. Both parks eventually feature swimming lagoons.

**1962** William Penn Mott Jr., former superintendent of parks for the City of Oakland, becomes the general manager. (Mott later serves as director of the California Department of Parks and Recreation and the National Park Service.) The Sunol Regional Wilderness is acquired.

**1964** A measure to annex most of Contra Costa County to the District is passed by 54 percent of voters. A $150 million statewide park bond also passes, allowing the District to acquire new parklands at Las Trampas, Little Hills, and Coyote Hills. The federal Wilderness Act passes.

**1965** The McAteer-Petris Act establishes the temporary Bay Conservation and Development Commission, the first coastal management agency in the nation.

**1966** The Association of Bay Area Governments publishes a preliminary regional plan for permanent open space. The Pleasanton area annexes to the District by a vote of 80 percent. The District now serves 1.7 million people. A lease agreement with the East Bay Municipal Utility District allows fishing and boating for the first time at Lake Chabot.

1967    The City of Alameda turns over part of Alameda State Beach (later renamed Robert W. Crown Memorial State Beach after the late assemblyman) to the District. Kennedy Grove Regional Recreation Area and Briones Regional Park open, the first two parks in Contra Costa County. Irwin Luckman succeeds William Penn Mott Jr. as general manager.

1968    Richard C. Trudeau becomes acting general manager (permanent in 1969), overseeing twenty parks, 22,000 acres, and a budget of nearly $12 million. The National Trail Systems Act is signed into law. People for Open Space publishes "The Case for Open Space" to follow on the Association of Bay Area Governments plan of 1966.

1969    The National Environmental Policy Act passes. The Association of Bay Area Governments publishes its first regional plan with a goal of 3.8 million acres of permanent open space. The now-permanent Bay Conservation and Development Commission establishes its San Francisco Bay Plan as state law. The Regional Parks Foundation is formed as a private, nonprofit corporation to support District programs and projects. Kaiser Industries donates a depleted quarry, and the new foundation transfers the land to the District to create the Shadow Cliffs Regional Recreation Area.

1970    The first Earth Day is celebrated in April. A $60 million state park bond is passed by 57 percent of voters in November. The California Environmental Quality Act passes, following upon the National Environmental Policy Act of 1969.

1971    The state legislature approves AB925, sponsored by John T. Knox, to allow the District a 10-cent tax increase for land acquisition, development, and operation. Save Mount Diablo is formed in Contra Costa County.

1972    The National Trails Council is established.

1973    Point Pinole Regional Shoreline opens at the site of a former explosives manufacturing plant (now a state historic landmark). The board adopts a comprehensive master plan created with the help of citizen committees and professional planners to emphasize "balanced acquisition" throughout the District's two counties.

This planning process results in a permanent Park Advisory Committee. The federal Endangered Species Act passes.

**1974** A $250 million state park bond passes with 60 percent approval in the June primary.

**1975** Portions of Black Diamond Mines Regional Preserve (formerly the largest coal producing site in California and later a center for underground sand mining) are acquired from the federal Bureau of Land Management. Morgan Territory Regional Preserve is created.

**1976** A $280 million state park bond is passed by 52 percent of voters in November. The first portion of the Martinez Regional Shoreline is acquired.

**1978** The statewide property tax revolt known as Proposition 13 passes in the June primary, altering finances for local government entities relying on property taxes.

**1979** The District cuts operating expenses by $1 million in response to property tax cuts of Proposition 13. San Leandro Bay Regional Shoreline (later renamed Martin Luther King Jr. Regional Shoreline), Brooks Island Regional Shoreline, and Point Isabel Regional Shoreline open, all managed by the District on leased land.

**1980** The District board adopts a revised master plan. Less than 10 percent of parklands will be developed, with the other 90 percent left in a natural condition. A $285 million state park bond passes in the November general election.

**1981** The portion of east Contra Costa County known as the Liberty Union High School District annexes to the East Bay Regional Park District.

**1982** The District establishes the Parks Express program to provide transportation to parks for at-risk youth, low-income seniors, and those with disabilities.

**1984** The District celebrates its 50th anniversary with 41 parks totaling 57,000 acres serving more than 15 million visitors. A $370 million state park bond passes in the June primary election.

**1985** General Manager Dick Trudeau retires and is succeeded by David E. Pesonen.

**1986**   Proposition 43, the Community Parklands Act, passes statewide at $100 million. Ardenwood Historic Farm opens in Fremont.

**1987**   The San Francisco Bay Trail is created by the state legislature with passage of SB100, sponsored by Senator Bill Lockyer.

**1988**   A $776 million statewide park bond (Proposition 70) passes in June. Round Valley Regional Preserve is acquired (opened to the public in 1998). The board adopts the revised "Master Plan 1989." Measure AA, a $225 million phased bond issue, passes in November to fund open space acquisition and recreational programs. Pat O'Brien is appointed to succeed David Pesonen as general manager. He begins work just days after the passage of Measure AA.

**1989**   The Bay Trail Plan is adopted by the Association of Bay Area Governments.

**1990**   The first thirty-four acres of the Bay Area Ridge Trail, running from Wildcat Canyon to Cull Canyon, are dedicated. The Bay Trail Project incorporates as a nonprofit.

**1991**   The East Bay hills firestorm in October destroys thousands of homes, also damaging Temescal Regional Recreation Area and Claremont Canyon Regional Preserve. The District creates an assessment district under the Landscape and Lighting Act of 1972 to fund operations at Round Valley and other parks in the fast-growing portion of east Contra Costa County annexed in 1981 without a tax base.

**1992**   The Livermore area of Alameda County known as Murray Township annexes to the District. After nearly sixty years, the District finally includes all of Alameda and Contra Costa counties.

**1993**   A second assessment district is formed under the Landscape and Lighting Act of 1972 to provide a local source of revenue for operation and maintenance of the District's extensive trail system throughout Alameda and Contra Costa counties.

**1994**   At its sixtieth anniversary, the District operates fifty public parklands and twenty regional trails totaling more than 76,000 acres.

**1995**   The Bay Area Open Space Council publishes "Open Space Vision" to map lands suitable for permanent protection. A memorial is dedicated at Briones Regional Park to honor Ivan Dickson, a longtime Berkeley Hiking Club member whose bequest of more than $427,000 to the District will fund volunteer trail maintenance.

**1996**   Voters approve Measures KK and LL by 78 and 67 percent, respectively, in the general election of November 5, authorizing continuance of Landscape and Lighting Act assessment districts funding District-wide trail maintenance (KK) and east Contra Costa County park operations (LL). The District's 1997 Master Plan is approved in December, saying: "An environmental ethic guides us in all that we do." The acquisition of Brushy Peak Regional Preserve begins.

**1997**   The District agrees to act as an agent of the State of California to purchase 1,430 acres from Catellus Corporation for Eastshore State Park. The purchase, completed in December 1998, passes the title from Catellus to a state/District joint powers authority. A joint project with the Contra Costa Water District acquires Vasco Caves Regional Preserve in east Contra Costa County.

**1998**   Measure W, the District's proposed parcel tax, fails to achieve the two-thirds majority required for passage in the November general election.

**1999**   At its sixty-fifth anniversary, the District comprises more than 91,000 acres with fifty-nine regional parklands and twenty-nine inter-park trails.

**2000**   An analysis of East Bay economic benefits shows that regional parks and trails contribute significantly to the quality of life. A $2.1 billion park and coastal protection bond passes statewide in March as Proposition 12.

**2001**   The three-phase purchase of 1,031-acre Clayton Ranch is completed to include part of a critical wildlife corridor between Mt. Diablo State Park and Black Diamond Mines Regional Preserve.
   Camp Arroyo, the residential environmental education and youth camp, opens near Del Valle in Livermore, in partnership with The Taylor Family Foundation. Quarry Lakes Regional Recreation Area opens as a joint project of the District, the Alameda County Water District, and the City of Fremont.

**2002**   Measure K, the District's proposed parcel tax (successor to Measure W), fails in the March primary. Voters pass the statewide Proposition 40, a $2.6 billion park and coastal protection bond, in the same election (the largest resource bond in U.S. history at that time).

2003    The Bay Area Ridge Trail surpasses 250 miles. The District's former headquarters on Skyline Boulevard is renamed the Richard C. Trudeau Training Center. Nicholl Knob, the highest peak at Miller/Knox Regional Shoreline, is dedicated in honor of local environmental advocate Lucretia Edwards.

2004    The District now includes 65 regional parks, more than 95,000 acres, and more than 1,100 miles of trails. The 772-acre Garaventa Property at Black Diamond Mines (formerly in land bank status) opens. Voters pass Measure CC, a fifteen-year parcel tax measure, in November (for infrastructure, habitat preservation, and fuels management in the District's western portion).
    The Regional Parks Foundation secures a $1.5 million grant from the Gordon and Betty Moore Foundation to acquire 617-acre Souza Property adjacent to Vasco Caves Regional Preserve, bringing Vasco Caves to 1,400 acres.

2005    The *San Francisco Business Times* names the District one of the 100 best places to work in the Bay Area. The District dedicates the 700-acre Sycamore Valley Regional Open Space in Danville and opens 1,700 acres of Brushy Peak Regional Preserve north of Livermore.

2006    Crockett Hills Regional Park opens in June, and the dedication ceremony includes the 300th mile of the Bay Area Ridge Trail.
    The District and the State of California dedicate Eastshore State Park and the completed Phase I restoration of Berkeley Meadow. The District collaborates on a reuse plan for the Concord Naval Weapons Station. Voters approve statewide Proposition 84, a $400 million park bond, in November.

2007    The 228-acre Chen property is purchased to expand Las Trampas Regional Wilderness. The California Coastal Conservancy awards a $1.5 million grant to fund final restoration of Berkeley Meadow. The 1,467-acre Tyler Ranch is acquired to expand Pleasanton Ridge Regional Park, the largest single land purchase in seventeen years. The board approves a new Master Plan Map.

**2008**  The District opens the nearly 150-acre Bay Point Regional Shoreline, and dedicates the mile-long Alameda Point at the former Alameda Naval Air Station.

On November 4, a $500 million bond extension, Measure WW, passes at 71.7 percent (the largest regional park bond ever passed nationwide).

**2009**  The District celebrates its seventy-fifth anniversary with public events throughout the regional parks. The board in partnership with the East Contra Costa County Habitat Conservation Conservancy buys 153 acres near Morgan Territory and 191 acres for the future Byron Vernal Pools Regional Preserve.

The 64-acre Chabot-Dunsmuir property is acquired with the City of Oakland, the first with Measure WW funds. In October, the District assumes title of 1,156 acres of Tyler Ranch to add to Pleasanton Ridge Regional Park, bringing the District's total land-holdings to 100,000 safely preserved acres, all within seventy-five years of the 1934 election that established the agency.

# Appendix 3

## Selected Legislation and Ballot Measures

**Note:** Items specific to the East Bay Regional Park District appear in *italics*.

1928    Proposition 4, the California State Park Bonds Act, is approved by voters as passed by the state legislature in 1927. It authorizes and directs the issuance and sale of $6 million in state bonds to acquire lands for state parks.

1933    *AB 1114 is signed into law by Governor James Rolph; it authorizes the establishment of a regional park district for Alameda and Contra Costa counties and a board to govern it.*

1964    State park bond of $150 million, the State Beach, Park, Recreational, and Historical Facilities Bond Act, passes with approval from 62 percent of voters.

1970    State park bond of $60 million, the Recreation and Fish and Wildlife Enhancement Act, passes with approval from 57 percent of voters in the November general election as Proposition 20.

1971    *AB 925, sponsored by Assemblyman John T. Knox, is approved by the state legislature and signed into law; it allows the District to obtain a 10-cent tax increase for parkland acquisition, development, and operation.*

1974    State park bond of $250 million passes with approval from 60 percent of voters in the June primary.

1976    State park bond of $280 million, the Nejedly-Hart State, Urban, and Coastal Park Bond Act, passes with approval from 52 percent of voters as Proposition 2 in the November general election.

1978    Proposition 13, the statewide property tax revolt, also known as the Jarvis-Gann initiative, passes in the June primary, dramatically changing funding of all local government entities that rely on property taxes.

1980    State park bond of $285 million, the California Parklands Act of 1980 authored by Senator John Nejedly, is approved by voters as Proposition 1 in the November general election.

**1984**  State park bond of $370 million, the California Park and Recreational Facilities Act, passes with approval from 63 percent of voters in the June primary as Proposition 18.

The $85 million Fish and Wildlife Habitat Enhancement Act is approved by 64 percent of voters as Proposition 19 in the June primary.

**1986**  Proposition 43, the Community Parklands Act of 1986, wins statewide passage in the June primary as a legislative initiative approved by 67 percent of voters to provide $100 million in grants for localities to acquire, develop, or rehabilitate park and recreational facilities.

Measure C, a Contra Costa County transportation measure tied to a half-cent increase in sales tax, fails in the November general election under opposition by some cities and open space advocates.

**1987**  Senate Bill 100, sponsored by Senator Bill Lockyer, creates a state-mandated plan for the San Francisco Bay Trail, a 500-mile trail system intended to surround the entire shoreline of San Francisco Bay.

**1988**  Proposition 70 passes in the June primary as the California Wildlife, Coastal, and Park Land Conservation Fund of 1988, a statewide bond approved by 65 percent of voters to provide $776 million for parks and wildlife. It was placed on the ballot as a citizen initiative by the Planning and Conservation League.

*Measure AA passes in the November general election to fund a $225 million phased bond issue for open space acquisition, recreational programs, and a grants program for cities and other local public agencies.*

Measure C, Contra Costa county's transportation measure, also passes in November as a companion to Measure AA (in both Alameda and Contra Costa counties). Measure C carries a half-cent sales tax increase and requires that those tax revenues be dedicated to county transportation projects and to the implementation of a Growth Management Initiative by all the cities and the county.

**1990**  A $437 million park bond, the California Park, Recreation, and Wildlife Act, fails by a 53 percent to 47 percent vote as Proposition 149 in the November general election.

**1994** A $2 billion measure, the Park Lands, Historic Sites, Wildlife, and Forest Conservation Bond Act, fails by a 57 percent to 43 percent vote in the June primary.

**1996** *Measure KK passes in November with approval by 78 percent of voters, authorizing continuance of the assessment district funding District-wide trail maintenance under the Landscape and Lighting Act.*

*Measure LL passes in November with the approval of 67 percent of voters to establish an assessment district under the Landscape and Lighting Act to fund East Contra Costa County park operations.*

**1998** Measure B goes before Alameda County voters in June, asking them to extend the existing Measure B, a one-half-cent transportation sales tax that would "sunset" in 2002. Although approved by more than 58 percent of voters, the measure does not muster the required two-thirds majority and is defeated.

*Measure W wins 65 percent of the "yes" vote (Alameda and Contra Costa counties) in the November election but fails to achieve the required two-thirds majority. The measure would have levied a parcel tax for infrastructure, habitat preservation, and fuels management. (See also Measure K, 2002, and Measure CC, 2004).*

**2000** Proposition 12 passes with approval from 63 percent of voters in the March primary as the Safe Neighborhood Parks, Clean Water, Clean Air, and Coastal Protection Bond Act of 2000, a $2.1 billion measure put on the ballot by the legislature as the Villaraigosa-Keeley Act.

Proposition 13 passes in the March primary as the Safe Drinking Water, Clean Water, Watershed Protection, and Flood Protection Bond Act. The $1.97 billion measure was placed on the ballot by the legislature.

Measure C fails in the November election for Alameda County. Chaired by former District board member Jocelyn Combs, it would have affirmed the county's existing urban growth boundary separating rural lands from those suitable for urban uses. Measure C is considered less restrictive than the competing Measure D on same ballot, which passed.

Measure D passes in November with 57 percent of the vote (and is later upheld by the First District Court of Appeal) to amend Alameda County's eastern urban growth boundary to allow less land for urban growth and more for agriculture and open space, a more restrictive prescription than that of the failed Measure C. It drew support from the Sierra Club and the Audubon Society.

2002    *Measure K receives a 62 percent "yes" vote in the March primary (Alameda and Contra Costa counties) but falls short of the two-thirds majority needed to pass. It is the second attempt after the similar Measure W in 1998. In 2004, Measure CC succeeds for a selected portion of the District.*

Proposition 40, a statewide $2.6 billion bond titled the California Clean Water, Clean Air, Safe Neighborhood Parks, and Coastal Protection Act of 2002, wins approval by 57 percent of voters in the March primary, representing the largest resource bond in U.S. history at that time.

Proposition 50, a major statewide water bond put on the ballot by citizen petition, passes in the November general election, providing $3.44 billion in general obligation bonds for "water quality, supply, and safe drinking water" and also coastal wetlands purchase and protection projects.

2004    *Measure CC passes in the November election, levying a 15-year parcel tax to raise some $3 million per year for infrastructure, habitat preservation, and fuels management in the western portion of the District (winning 67.6 percent of the vote in the cities of Alameda, Albany, Berkeley, El Cerrito, Emeryville, Kensington, Oakland, Piedmont, San Pablo, and part of Pinole). Measure CC follows the failed Measures W (1998) and K (2002), which would have covered the District's full territory.*

2006    In November California voters approve Proposition 84, a $400 million statewide park bond, later followed up by legislative action to ensure funding would reach underserved communities.

2008    *Measure WW passes in the November general election with 71 percent approval of voters in Alameda and Contra Costa counties combined, representing a $500 million bond extension of the earlier Measure AA (1988), at no increase in tax rate. It is the largest such regional park bond ever passed in the U.S.*

# Selected Sources

**Books**

*A Vision Achieved: Fifty Years of East Bay Regional Park District*, by Mimi Stein. Oakland: East Bay Regional Park District, 1984.

*After the Storm: Bob Walker and the East Bay Regional Park District*, by Christopher Beaver. Berkeley: Wilderness Press, 2007.

*Berkeley: A City in History*, by Charles Wollenberg. Berkeley: University of California Press, 2007. Online at www.berkeleypubliclibrary.org/system/historytext.html.

*The Country in the City: The Greening of the San Francisco Bay Area*, by Richard A. Walker. Seattle: University of Washington Press, 2007.

*The East Bay Out: A Personal Guide to the East Bay Regional Parks*, by Malcolm Margolin. Berkeley: Heyday Books, 1988.

*East Bay Trails: Hiking Trails in Alameda and Contra Costa Counties*, by David Weintraub. Berkeley: Wilderness Press, 2005.

*Guide to the Plant Species of the Regional Parks Botanic Garden*, by James B. Roof. Oakland: East Bay Regional Park District, 1959.

*Its Name Was M.U.D.*, by John Wesley Noble. Oakland: East Bay Municipal Utility District, 1970.

*Land Conservation Financing*, by Mike McQueen and Ed McMahon. Washington: Island Press, 2003.

*Preserving the Nation: The Conservation and Environmental Movements*, 1870–2000, by Thomas R. Wellock. Wheeling, IL: Harlan Davidson, Inc., 2007.

*Prophet of the Parks: The Story of William Penn Mott Jr.*, by Mary Ellen Butler. Ashburn, VA: National Recreation and Parks Association, 1989.

*Saving Open Space: The Politics of Local Preservation in California*, by Daniel Press. Berkeley: University of California Press, 2002.

*Special Districts in California Local Government*, by Stanley Scott and John C. Bollens. Berkeley: Bureau of Public Administration, University of California, 1949.

## Manuscripts, Documents, and Archival Collections

August Vollmer papers. Bancroft Library, University of California, Berkeley.

"Creating the Eastshore State Park: An Activist History." (manuscript) Norman La Force, 2002.

"The Diablo Ridgelands: Protecting and Enhancing a Regional Landscape," Diablo Ridgelands Working Group, Bay Area Open Space Council, July 2002.

"The Early Story of the East Bay Regional Parks." Elbert M. Vail, East Bay Regional Park District, 1942.

"The East Bay Hills Fire," U.S. Fire Administration/Technical Report Series (USFA-TR-060/October 1991).

"The East Bay Regional Park District." (UC Berkeley dissertation) Albert Raeburn, 1943.

"The East Bay Regional Park Story." East Bay Regional Park District, 1954.

"Fact Sheet: The ERAF Property Tax Shift." League of California Cities, September 2008.

"A Historical Sketch and Analytical View of the East Bay Regional Park District in Alameda County." (report of the general manager) Richard E. Walpole, 1958.

"History: East Bay Regional Park District, 1934–1975." Richard C. Trudeau, East Bay Regional Park District, 1975.

"Park and Trail Statistics," (annual) Land Division, East Bay Regional Park District.

"A Park for the People: Origins of the East Bay Regional Park District." (manuscript) Pete Ahrens, 2006.

"Park Politics: The East Bay Regional Park District, a Study of Bay Area Intergovernmental Relations and Delivery of Public Services." (University of California, Berkeley thesis) Elisabeth A. Garratt, 1983.

"The Property Tax Roller Coaster: Explanations for Variations in County Property Tax Revenues." California State Association of Counties, October 2004.

"Report of the Blue Ribbon Urban Interface Fire Prevention Committee," February 1982.

Richard C. Trudeau papers. Bancroft Library, University of California, Berkeley.

"Ridgelands: A Multijurisdictional Open Space Study," Alameda, Contra Costa, and Santa Clara counties, East Bay Regional Park District, Association of Bay Area Governments, and U.S. Bureau of Outdoor Recreation, May 1977.

Robert Sibley papers. Bancroft Library, University of California, Berkeley.

Samuel C. May papers. Bancroft Library, University of California, Berkeley.

"Tenth Anniversary Report of the East Bay Regional Park District." Richard E. Walpole, General Manager, East Bay Regional Park District, 1945.

"The Tunnel Incident, Oakland 1991, Ten Years After," Hills Emergency Forum, October 3, 2001.

William Penn Mott Jr. Memorial Fund records, 1943–2001. Bancroft Library, University of California, Berkeley.


## Oral Histories

"A View of the Park District from the Board of Directors, 1958–1976." Oral history of Clyde R. Woolridge conducted by Carole Hicke in 1981. Bancroft Library, University of California, Berkeley.

"Attorney and Activist for the Environment." Oral history of David E. Pesonen conducted by Ann Lage in 1991–1992. Bancroft Library, University of California, Berkeley.

"Dramatic Growth in Changing Times: Recollections of the General Manager." Oral history of Richard C. Trudeau conducted by Mimi Stein in 1982. East Bay Regional Park District.

"Dynamic Park Leadership, 1962–1967." Oral history of William Penn Mott Jr. conducted by Mimi Stein in 1981. East Bay Regional Park District.

"From Skyline to Seashore: Twenty-Two Years of Leadership, Land Acquisition, and Lobbying at the East Bay Regional Park District, 1964–1986." Oral history of Richard C. Trudeau conducted by Laura McCreery in 2001. Bancroft Library, University of California, Berkeley.

"Services for Californians: Executive Department in the Reagan Administration, 1967–1974." Includes oral history of William Penn Mott Jr. conducted by Ann Lage in 1984. Bancroft Library, University of California, Berkeley.

Series of oral histories conducted by Mimi Stein and Carole Hicke for the East Bay Regional Park District in the early 1980s. In addition to the interviews with Trudeau and Mott, listed separately above, the series included dozens of other interviewees, such as Donn Black, Joseph P. Bort, George H. Cardinet Jr., Howard C. Cogswell, Paul E. Harberts, Hulet Hornbeck, Mary Lee Jefferds, John T. Knox, John J. Leavitt, Jerry D. Kent, Kay Kerr, Georgette Morton, John A. Nejedly, O. Christian Nelson, Glenn T. Seaborg, Carol Sibley, and Clyde R. Woodridge.

# Notes

This appendix provides notes about sources for each chapter (by page number and phrase in text).

## Chapter 1

1 **In spite of the** *Oakland Tribune*, January 30, 1931, p. 23. The Hotel Oakland was at 260 13th Street.

2 **Frederick Law Olmsted Sr.** Olmsted Brothers, East Bay Regional Park Association, and University of California, Berkeley. 1930. "Proposed Park Reservations for East Bay Cities, California." Berkeley: Bureau of Public Administration, University of California, pp. 15–16; John Wesley Noble and East Bay Municipal Utility District. *Its Name Was M.U.D.* East Bay Municipal Utility District, 1970, p. 57.

2 **In the early twentieth century** Albert Raeburn. The East Bay Regional Park District, 1943, p. 6; Olmsted Brothers, p. 16.

2 **Since the 1860s** Noble, pp. 3–4.

2 **A severe drought during** Noble, pp. 19–20.

2 **After passage of enabling legislation** Elisabeth A. Garratt. "Park Politics: The East Bay Regional Park District, a Study of Bay Area Intergovernmental Relations and Delivery of Public Services," 1983, pp. 12–13.

2 **The importance of a reliable** Charles Wollenberg. *Berkeley: A City in History*. Berkeley: University of California Press, 2008, Chapter 6; "Response of the San Francisco Fire Department to the Berkeley Conflagration of September 17, 1923." Virtual Museum of the City of San Francisco at www.sfmuseum.org/oakfire/berkeley.html.

2 **In 1928, five years after** Olmsted Brothers, p. 17.

2 **Suddenly some 10,000 acres** Letter from George Pardee of East Bay Municipal Utility District, January 10, 1931. Samuel C. May papers, Bancroft Library.

3 **Although builders and developers** Garratt, p. 8.

3 **Such a result could be achieved** Raeburn, p. 7.

3 **... an alliance of park and recreation groups petitioned** Raeburn, pp. 7–8.

3 **In 1929, the same year** Noble, pp. 163, 57.

3 **Robert Sibley, a University of California** Noble, pp. 163, 57.

3 **Sibley already had approached** Robert Sibley papers, Bancroft Library.

3 **At Sibley's suggestion** Noble, pp. 163, 57.

3 **"The East Bay communities face ..."** Olmsted Brothers, p. 40.

5    ... had its first thousand signatures  *Oakland Post-Enquirer, Oakland Tribune, Richmond Independent, Berkeley Gazette*, January 30, 1931.

5    **Representatives of nine city governments**  Mary Ellen Butler. *Prophet of the Parks: The Story of William Penn Mott, Jr.* Ashburn, VA: National Recreation and Park Association, 1999, p. 70; The nine cities were Alameda, Albany, Berkeley, El Cerrito, Emeryville, Oakland, Piedmont, Richmond, and San Leandro.

5    **"Persuasion went on for some time"**  Raeburn, pp. 9–10.

5    **Pardee justified the decision in writing**  Raeburn, p. 10; letter from George Pardee of East Bay Municipal Utility District, January 10, 1931. Samuel C. May Papers, Bancroft Library.

5    **In spite of dissent from some**  Mimi Stein. *A Vision Achieved: Fifty Years of East Bay Regional Park District*. East Bay Regional Park District, 1984, p. 8.

5    **Mayors of the East Bay cities**  Raeburn, p. 12; Stein, p. 9.

5    **But Frank Mott, a former Oakland mayor**  William Penn Mott. "Dynamic Park Leadership, 1962–1967." Oral history interview conducted by Mimi Stein in 1981, pp. 3–4; Raeburn, p. 12; Stein, p. 9. The bill was AB 1114.

6    **The cities of El Cerrito and Richmond**  *Oakland Tribune*, October 2, 1934, p. 35; Butler, p. 70; Stein, p. 9.

6    **Within weeks of the election**  East Bay Regional Park District. The East Bay Regional Park Story, 1954.

6    **... the board looked again to the Oakland Planning Commissioner**  Raeburn, p. 29; Stein, p. 14.

6    **The new District did buy**  Stein, pp. 14–15.

6    **By 1936 a compromise**  Stein, p. 15.

7    **In a spirit of great celebration**  Stein, pp. 15–16.

7    **General Manager Vail**  Raeburn, pp. 29–30; Stein, pp. 16–18.

7    **Tilden Park quickly became**  Stein, p. 20.

7    **Meanwhile, the board and skeleton staff**  Stein, p. 23.

7    **Despite the effects of the Great Depression**  Stein, pp. 25–26.

8    **With the bombing of**  Stein, pp. 29–32.

8    **When Vail resigned**  Raeburn, pp. 30–33; Stein, pp. 30, 32.

8    **"He was hired as a laborer ..."**  Georgette Morton. The East Bay Regional Park District's First Girl Friday. Oral history interview conducted by Mimi Stein in 1980, p. 19.

8    **Richard Walpole had been hired**  Author interview in 2009 with Jerry Kent, who had learned biographical details from Walpole's daughter.

8    **In 1946 the board restored**  Stein, pp. 35–37.

9    **New parcels increased the size**  Stein, pp. 37–39.

9    **By its 20th anniversary**  Stein, pp. 45–46.

9    **Residents of nearby Eden**  Stein, p. 39; Butler, p. 56.

9    **Trained as a landscape architect**  Butler, p. 16.

9    **As superintendent of parks**  Butler, Chapter 2.

9    **"This ability to squeeze water ..."**  Butler, p. 18.

10    **In 1960 Sproul suggested**  Butler, pp. 57–59, 74.

10    **Once hired, Mott applied the vigorous**  Butler, pp. 55, 59–62.

10    **Mott "wanted to know what you did ..."**  Butler, p. 60.

10    **"He insisted on excellence ..."**  Butler, p. 62.

10    **While Mott maintained**  Butler, p. 62.

10    **Mott combined a personal touch**  Butler, p. 63. The present-day union is the East Bay Regional Park Employees, Local 2428 of AFSCME, AFL-CIO.

10    **When he decided in 1965**  Butler, pp. 65, 73; Stein, p. 67; Richard C. Trudeau. "From Skyline to Seashore: Twenty-Two Years of Leadership, Land Acquisition, and Lobbying at the East Bay Regional Park District, 1964–1986." Oral history interview conducted by Laura McCreery in 2001. Bancroft Library, pp. 83–85.

10    **Rather than disband**  *The Bay Leaf*, California Native Plant Society (East Bay Chapter), January 2006.

11    **... Mott reviewed the small**  Butler, pp. 60–61; Stein, pp. 67–68.

11    **With key aid from state legislators**  Stein, p. 52; Trudeau oral history, 2001, p. 115.

11    **A capstone of Mott's tenure**  Mott oral history, 1981; Trudeau oral history, 2001; Butler, pp. 70–73; Stein, pp. 48–51. The grassroots campaign to annex Contra Costa County was organized as Citizens for Regional Parks NOW with Dr. Clark Kerr and Catherine "Kay" Kerr as honorary cochairs.

11    **As county counsel and district attorney**  John A. Nejedly. "A State Senator's Contribution to the Park District." Oral history interview conducted by Mimi Stein in 1982.

11    **Through that campaign**  Trudeau oral history, 2001.

12    **The growing tax base**  Stein, p. 51.

12    **... Mott moved quickly**  Stein, pp. 52–53.

12    **With funding from a 1965**  Stein, pp. 53–54; Trudeau oral history, 2001, pp. 89–91. The bond issue followed passage of a $150-million state park bond in the November 1964 general election.

12    **"Coyote Hills was the big one ..."**  Trudeau oral history, 2001, p. 89.

12    **Several years of negotiations**  Stein, p. 55.

12   **With land acquisition a top priority**  Butler, pp. 66–70; Hulet Hornbeck. Park District Acquisitions, 1965–1981. Oral history interview conducted by Carole Hicke in 1981.

12   **"Hulet was an interesting . . ."**  Trudeau oral history, 2001, p. 78.

12   **Mott himself believed strongly**  Butler, p. 66.

12   **After rebuilding beaches**  Stein, p. 60.

12   **When Save the Bay**  Butler, pp. 76–77, 87; Stein, pp. 56–59.

13   **Governor Ronald Reagan too**  *Los Angeles Times*, February 15, 1967, p. 24; Butler, pp. 77, 81–85.

13   **Suddenly the District's "Mott era"**  Stein, p. 69; Butler, pp. 77–79.

## Chapter 2

15   **By promoting Mott's planning and design chief**  Richard C. Trudeau. "From Skyline to Seashore: Twenty-Two Years of Leadership, Land Acquisition, and Lobbying at the East Bay Regional Park District, 1964–1986." Oral history interview conducted by Laura McCreery in 2001. Bancroft Library, pp. 95–98; Richard C. Trudeau. "Dramatic Growth in Changing Times: Recollections of the General Manager." Oral history conducted by Mimi Stein in 1982. East Bay Regional Park District, pp. 32–34; Mimi Stein. *A Vision Achieved: Fifty Years of East Bay Regional Park District*. East Bay Regional Park District, 1984, p. 69.

15   **Like Mott, Luckman**  Author interview in 2009 with Jerry Kent.

15   **He had created the first**  Stein, pp. 60–61; Mary Ellen Butler. *Prophet of the Parks: The Story of William Penn Mott Jr*. Ashburn, VA: National Recreation and Park Association, 1999, p. 68.

15   **. . . he resigned after only a year**  Trudeau oral history, 2001, p. 98; Stein, pp. 69–70.

16   **The board quickly promoted**  Trudeau oral history, 2001, pp. 98–100.

16   **Trudeau had been**  Trudeau oral history, 2001.

16   **After the park's opening in 1968**  *New York Times*, December 15, 1968.

17   **Adjacent to Sunol Regional Wilderness**  Trudeau oral history, 1982, pp. 39–45; Trudeau oral history, 2001, pp. 102–107; Stein, pp. 71–75.

17   **The *Oakland Tribune* later quoted**  *Oakland Tribune*, November 24, 2004.

17   **To fund these ambitious plans**  Trudeau oral history, 2001, pp. 115–118; Stein, pp. 78–79. The legislation was Knox's AB 925.

18   **"I guess we spent about a year . . ."**  Joseph P. Bort. "Recollections of the Chairman of the Board, Alameda County Board of Supervisors." Oral history interview conducted by Mimi Stein in 1982.

18   **Armed with federal funds**  Stein, p. 80.

18   **By designating each parcel**  East Bay Regional Park District. 1973. Master Plan.

18    **The District took the unprecedented step**  Stein, pp. 80, 82.

19    **As an added benefit**  Stein, p. 83.

19    **With a key goal**  Stein, pp. 56–59, 84–88.

21    **He introduced a new method**  Trudeau oral history, 2001, p. 210.

21    **In 1974 the board commissioned**  Stein, p. 98. Arthur Young and Co. conducted the study.

21    **… an early adopter of an affirmative action program**  Trudeau oral history, 2001, pp. 137–142; Stein, p. 99.

21    **But a labor strike in 1975**  Trudeau oral history, 2001, pp. 154–161; Stein, pp. 99–100.

22    **The morning after the election**  Trudeau oral history, 2001, p. 183.

22    **Faced with the loss**  Trudeau oral history, 2001, pp. 183–187; Stein, p. 103.

22    **One innovation growing directly**  Trudeau oral history, 2001, pp. 183, 187–189; Stein, pp. 103–104.

22    **In the late sixties**  Trudeau oral history, 2001, pp. 102, 168, 245.

22    **He tapped John Zierold**  Trudeau oral history, 1982, pp. 24, 50, 104; Trudeau oral history, 2001, p. 120; Stein, p. 104.

23    **A revision, adopted in 1980**  East Bay Regional Park District. Master Plan. 1980.

23    **Director Ted Radke led a search**  Author interview in 2009 with Ted Radke; Trudeau oral history, 2001, pp. 120, 214.

23    **With the long-sought annexation**  Trudeau oral history, 1982, p. 17; Stein, p. 51.

**Chapter 3**

27    **Even before Hulet Hornbeck hired on**  Hulet Hornbeck. "Park District Acquisitions, 1965–1981." Oral history interview conducted by Carole Hicke in 1981. This interview is the source of all direct quotes by Hornbeck in Chapter 3, unless otherwise noted, as well as much of the background material about his life and career.

28    **"When you're buying land for parks …"**  William Penn Mott. "Dynamic Park Leadership, 1962–1967." Oral history interview conducted by Mimi Stein in 1981, p. 14.

30    **"He was smart enough …"**  John A. Nejedly. "A State Senator's Contribution to the Park District." Oral history interview conducted by Mimi Stein in 1982, p. 19.

30    **"He would always show up …"**  Nejedly oral history, 1982, p. 19.

30    **Understated, even taciturn, he "kept a low …"**  *Contra Costa Times*, November 21, 2005.

31    **Several active hiking clubs**  Mimi Stein. *A Vision Achieved: Fifty Years of East Bay Regional Park District*. East Bay Regional Park District, 1984, pp. 5, 10.

31    **Mott, too, had pushed**  Mott oral history, 1981; Trudeau oral history, 1982, pp. 65–68.

34   **Cardinet was ...“godfather of cross-state ...”**  Author interview in 2009 with Bob Doyle.

35   **A young ranger at the newly opened**  Author interview in 2009 with Doyle.

36   **“We want to keep you here ...”**  Author interview in 2009 with Doyle.

36   **“Western Electric intended to sell ...”**  Author interview in 2009 with Doyle.

36   **... board members Mary Jefferds and Harlan Kessel**  Mary Lee Jefferds. “Recollections of a Park District Director in the ’70s and ’80s.” Oral history interview conducted by Mimi Stein in 1982, pp. 12–16.

37   **... nearly 300 other private parcels**  Author interview in 2009 with Doyle.

37   **... Assemblyman Tom Bates carried legislation**  Trudeau oral history, 1982, p. 134.

37   **As Jefferds phrased it**  Lifestyle supplement to the *Hills Newspapers/East Bay Daily News*, December 1, 2006.

## Chapter 4

40   **A telephone survey conducted by an outside firm**  Tyler Research Associates. 1976. *The East Bay Regional Park District Need and Demand Survey: A Two-Phase Research Study*. San Francisco: Tyler Research Associates.

40   **Hulet Hornbeck called it “a wonderful experience”**  *San Francisco Chronicle*, November 27, 2004, p. B-5.

40   **“It was a very split board ...”**  Author interview in 2009 with Jerry Kent.

40   **In the mold of Bill Mott**  Richard C. Trudeau.  “From Skyline to Seashore: Twenty-Two Years of Leadership, Land Acquisition, and Lobbying at the East Bay Regional Park District, 1964–1986.” Oral history interview conducted by Laura McCreery in 2001. Bancroft Library.

41   **“He was a fighter ...”**  Author interview in 2009 with Kent.

41   **Among them were several park professionals**  Pat O’Brien. “An Entrepreneur for the Environment: Creative Leadership of the East Bay Regional Park District and Four Decades in California’s Local Park and Recreation Agencies, 1968–2008.” Oral history interview conducted by Laura McCreery in 2008–2009. Bancroft Library.

41   **Director Harlan Kessel**  Trudeau oral history, 2001, pp. 211–212.

41   **... the board appointed him general manager**  Author interview in 2009 with James H. Duncan, former director of Ward 4. Duncan recalled the board’s vote of 6–1, noting that he was the lone dissenter but was later persuaded to make the appointment unanimous.

42   **Pesonen, an attorney who also**  David E. Pesonen. “Attorney and Activist for the Environment, 1962–1992.” Oral history interview conducted by Ann Lage in 1991–1992. Bancroft Library. This interview is the source of all direct quotes by him in Chapter 4, as well as much of the background material about his life and career.

42 **That document, known today** "The wilderness letter" is available on the web site of the Wilderness Society at http://wilderness.org.

43 **Upon arriving for work in the morning** Author interview in 2009 with Rosemary Cameron.

43 **"In Sacramento, the governor . . ."** Trudeau oral history, 2001.

43 **"That $17 million 'loan' for land . . ."** Author interview in 2009 with Kent.

44 **He did elevate the role of planning** Author interview in 2009 with Ted Radke.

45 **"I don't like what general managers . . ."** Author interview in 2009 with Kent.

45 **The board sought out other candidates (and pp. 45–51)** O'Brien oral history, 2008–2009.

## Chapter 5

53 **In Sacramento, Pat O'Brien had worked** Author interview in 2009 with Pat O'Brien.

53 **Dick Trudeau, the District's former . . .** Richard C. Trudeau. "From Skyline to Seashore: Twenty-Two Years of Leadership, Land Acquisition, and Lobbying at the East Bay Regional Park District, 1964–1986." Oral history interview conducted by Laura McCreery in 2001. Bancroft Library.

55 **Kent had attended** Jerry D. Kent. "Recollections of the Assistant General Manager." Oral history interview conducted by Mimi Stein in 1982; author interview in 2009 with Kent.

55 **But in early June 1988** Author interviews in 2009 with Kent and Ted Radke.

56 **As an exploratory step** Agenda, Special Information Meeting, June 14, 1988.

57 **With some 6,000 new homes** Author interview in 2009 with Doyle.

57 **Kent's reluctance about the bond** Author interview in 2009 with Kent.

57 **Radke had advised** Author interview in 2009 with Radke.

58 **As board president, Jefferds** Approved Minutes, Regular Board Meeting of June 21, 1988; East Bay Regional Park District Resolution No. 1988-6-230, June 21, 1988.

59 **A volunteer campaign committee** Author interview in 2009 with Kent.

59 **On his own, Evanoff** "Miscellaneous Information" attached to board materials by Public Affairs: "On May 12, 1988, Mark Evanoff of People for Open Space sent a letter to cities in the two counties asking for a possible project list . . ."

59 **"For 47 cents a month . . ."** This slogan appeared on Measure AA campaign materials.

59 **Bob Doyle, who had succeeded Hornbeck** Author interviews in 2009 with Doyle and Kent.

60 **Meeting on July 5, 1988** Approved Minutes, Regular Board Meeting of July 5, 1988.

60 **George Manross and his associate** "Study to Determine the Feasibility for Approval of a $200–$400 Million Bond Measure in November '88 Election," Strategy Research Institute, July 1988.

61 **Finally, Director Combs urged serious consideration** Author interview in 2009 with Combs and informal discussions in 2009 with Kent and Radke.

61 **The Park Advisory Committee addressed** According to the board's Approved Minutes for July 19, 1988, Chuck Lewis reported the PAC's "about 50/50" [percent] split; the actual vote of members appears elsewhere (and is recalled by Kent) as 11–11.

61 **Nevertheless, the board unanimously** East Bay Regional Park District Resolution No. 1988-7-263, July 19, 1988.

61 **On August 2, Kent and his staff** Approved Minutes, Regular Board Meeting of August 2, 1988; East Bay Regional Park District Ordinance No. 1988-8-279, August 2, 1988.

62 **The world-champion rodeo cowboy** "Sharing a Vision: The Story of Measure AA" by Mark Evanoff (copy of typed manuscript with penciled notation "Mark's original version"). The nearly identical text was later published as "General Obligation Bond Funding for Parks & Open Space: The Story of Measure AA" in *Western Governmental Researcher* [Vol. VI, Nos. 1 & 2 (1990)] with the byline "Janet Cobb, Assistant General Manager, East Bay Regional Park District."

62 **"I'm not bragging . . ."** "Who is Jack Roddy?" www.roddyranch.com.

62 **. . . Janet Cobb surprised Kent** Author interview in 2009 with Kent.

63 **Measure AA had won** *Contra Costa Times*, November 19, 1988, p. 1A.

## Chapter 6

65 **In spite of the challenges ahead (and pp. 65–67)** Pat O'Brien. "An Entrepreneur for the Environment: Creative Leadership of the East Bay Regional Park District and Four Decades in California's Local Park and Recreation Agencies, 1968–2008." Oral history interview conducted by Laura McCreery in 2008–2009. Bancroft Library.

67 **Raised in Berkeley,** Mary Lee Jefferds. "Recollections of a Park District Director in the '70s and '80s." Oral history interview conducted by Mimi Stein in 1982.

67 **"In the early 1930s . . ."** From Es Anderson's article on web site of Tilden-Wildcat Horsemen's Association at www.twha.org/articles/articles.html.

68 **Jefferds's twenty-year environmental** Jefferds oral history, 1982.

68 **"The legislators . . . said . . ."** Richard C. Trudeau. "From Skyline to Seashore: Twenty-Two Years of Leadership, Land Acquisition, and Lobbying at the East Bay Regional Park District, 1964–1986." Oral history interview conducted by Laura McCreery in 2001. Bancroft Library.

69 **"Everybody knew I had no . . ."** Paul E. Harberts. "A Director's Recollections, 1968–1972." Oral history interview conducted by Carole Hicke in 1982.

69    **"I won, which was a great shock ..."** Jefferds oral history, 1982.

72    **"She believed in a hands-on approach ..."** Trudeau oral history, 2001.

72    **By the time O'Brien became** Author interviews in 2009 with Radke and Kent.

73    **"When I got here ..."** O'Brien oral history, 2009.

74    **Simultaneous to board and bond matters** O'Brien oral history, 2009.

75    **"The distribution outside this elite ..."** Author interview in 2009 with Rosemary Cameron.

75    **Another of O'Brien's priorities (and pp. 75–77)** O'Brien oral history, 2009.


**Chapter 7**

79    **Nearly twenty years after the fact** Esther Gulick quote and general story pp. 60–61 from the Horace M. Albright Lecture delivered jointly by Gulick, Catherine Kerr, and Sylvia McLaughlin at Berkeley, California, on April 14, 1988: "Saving San Francisco Bay: Past, Present, and Future," http://nature.berkeley.edu/site/lectures/albright/1988.php.

82    **During Mott's tenure as general manager** William Penn Mott. "Dynamic Park Leadership, 1962–1967." Oral history interview conducted by Mimi Stein in 1981; Richard C. Trudeau. "Dramatic Growth in Changing Times: Recollections of the General Manager." Oral history conducted by Mimi Stein in 1982. East Bay Regional Park District, pp. 69–78.

82    **As Mott's right hand** Richard C. Trudeau. "From Skyline to Seashore: Twenty-Two Years of Leadership, Land Acquisition, and Lobbying at the East Bay Regional Park District, 1964–1986." Oral history interview conducted by Laura McCreery in 2001, pp. 127–131. Bancroft Library; Mimi Stein. *A Vision Achieved: Fifty Years of East Bay Regional Park District*. East Bay Regional Park District, 1984, pp. 84–87.

83    **Much of the groundwork** Author interview in 2009 with Bob Doyle; Trudeau oral history, 1982, p. 87.

83    **The first was Miller/Knox** Stein, 1984, p. 87.

84    **"That's an example ..."** Pat O'Brien. "An Entrepreneur for the Environment: Creative Leadership of the East Bay Regional Park District and Four Decades in California's Local Park and Recreation Agencies, 1968–2008." Oral history interview conducted by Laura McCreery in 2008–2009. Bancroft Library.

84    **Just a few miles south** Stein, 1984, p. 89.

85    **"It took years ..."** Author interview in 2009 with John Sutter, 2009.

85    **When public access at last** Stein, 1984, p. 88.

85    **More than a decade later** Author interviews in 2009 with Mike Anderson and Pat O'Brien, 2009; O'Brien oral history, 2009.

86    **Creation of the Martinez Regional Shoreline**  Author interview in 2009 with Ted Radke.

86    **When the Santa Fe Railway**  Norman La Force. "Creating the Eastshore State Park: An Activist History." 2002.

87    **The proposed park did appear**  O'Brien oral history, 2008–2009.

87    **… a coalition of environmental organizations**  La Force, 2002.

88    **"He was going to run a bill …"**  O'Brien oral history, 2008–2009.

90    **The Point Pinole area returned to the spotlight**  Author interviews in 2009 with O'Brien and Doyle; O'Brien oral history, 2009.

## Chapter 8

95    **Outside the main building**  Author interviews in 2009 with Frances Heath, Darrell Jones, and Jerry Kent.

96    **The East Bay as a whole**  Significant sources of detail about the 1991 firestorm include "The East Bay Hills Fire," U.S. Fire Administration/Technical Report Series (USFA-TR-060/October 1991) and "The Tunnel Incident, Oakland 1991, Ten Years After," Hills Emergency Forum, October 3, 2001.

96    **The District had emphasized fire prevention**  March 1936. Walker B. Tilley. General Fire Plan, Proposed East Bay Regional Park.

97    **By 1973, with 1,300 square miles**  Mimi Stein. *A Vision Achieved: Fifty Years of East Bay Regional Park District*. East Bay Regional Park District, 1984, p. 101.

97    **The much-maligned eucalyptus**  "Ubiquitous Eucalyptus: How an Aussie Got Naturalized." *Bay Nature*, July–September 2005.

97    **In the aftermath of an extraordinary**  Richard C. Trudeau. "From Skyline to Seashore: Twenty-Two Years of Leadership, Land Acquisition, and Lobbying at the East Bay Regional Park District, 1964–1986." Oral history interview conducted by Laura McCreery in 2001. Bancroft Library; Stein, p. 103.

98    **Filing a 100-page report**  1982 Report of the Blue Ribbon Urban Interface Fire Prevention Committee, adopted by the East Bay Regional Park District board as Resolution 1982-2-44 on February 2, 1982.

98    **"We included many important …"**  Author interview in 2009 with Kent.

98    **In October 1991, nearly ten years**  Author interview in 2009 with Kent.

98    **As a founding member**  Author interviews in 2009 with O'Brien and Kent.

101   **In 1994, four**  RAWS information is available at www.ebparks.org/about/fire/raws.

101   **In 2009, after three years**  East Bay Regional Park District Wildfire Hazard Reduction and Resource Management Plan Environmental Impact Report, July 2009.

101    **The first occurred at Shell Marsh**  Author interviews in 2009 with O'Brien and Radke.

101    **The second oil spill**  Author interview in 2009 with O'Brien; East Bay Regional Park District Comprehensive Annual Financial Report for the Year Ended December 31, 2007. The regional parks that were partially closed after the *Cosco Busan* oil spill were Brooks Island, Point Pinole, Miller/Knox, Point Isabel, Eastshore State Park, Middle Harbor, and Crown Beach.

103    **. . . the District's public safety division patrols**  Author communication in 2009 with Tim Anderson; East Bay Regional Park District web site pages for police and fire departments.

103    **Assistant General Manager Mike Anderson**  Author interview in 2009 with Mike Anderson.

106    **"When the Europeans first came here . . ."**  Pat O'Brien. "An Entrepreneur for the Environment: Creative Leadership of the East Bay Regional Park District and Four Decades in California's Local Park and Recreation Agencies, 1968–2008." Oral history interview conducted by Laura McCreery in 2008–2009. Bancroft Library.

107    **"In the Martinez fire of 2004 . . ."**  Author interview in 2009 with Ted Radke.

107    **"There was a time when we really didn't . . ."**  O'Brien oral history, 2008–2009.

107    **"A lot of the land . . ."**  Author interview in 2009 with Ayn Wieskamp.

107    **The Grasslands Monitoring Project**  A project of University of California, Berkeley's Department of Environmental Science, Policy, and Management under the leadership of Professors James W. Bartolome and Reginald H. Barrett, principal investigators.

107    **"We've put a lot of science . . ."**  O'Brien oral history, 2008–2009.

### Chapter 9

111    **"The board had just written it off" (pp. 111–113)**  Pat O'Brien. "An Entrepreneur for the Environment: Creative Leadership of the East Bay Regional Park District and Four Decades in California's Local Park and Recreation Agencies, 1968–2008." Oral history interview conducted by Laura McCreery in 2008–2009. Bancroft Library.

118    **But within a few years, board member Ted Radke**  Author interview in 2009 with Radke.

119    **"Without these funds . . ."**  East Bay Regional Park District press release, August 12, 1996.

119    **"The state budget crises . . ." (and pp. TK–TK)**  O'Brien oral history, 2008–2009.

121    **The economic woes of the early 1990s**  O'Brien oral history, 2008–2009; author interview in 2009 with Jerry Kent.

121    **"Land doesn't protect itself . . ."**  *San Francisco Chronicle*, October 31, 1998, p. A-17.

123    **In all, ten people signed**  Alameda County ballot pamphlet, November 1998 general election.

124 **Although the measure won** *San Francisco Chronicle*, November 5, 1998, p. A-26. On November 6, the *Chronicle* published former board member Harlan Kessel's letter to the editor (signed on behalf of Friends of Parks El Cerrito) thanking voters for defeating Measure W. Three other former board members, John O'Donnell, James Duncan, and Oliver Holmes, wrote a follow-up letter to the editor excoriating Kessel for opposing the measure. "East Bay residents should keep Mr. Kessel and his few followers in mind when the lack of funding for necessary maintenance of regional parks and trails takes its inevitable toll . . ." They wrote. "Mr. Kessel is no friend of parks."

124 **In the primary election of March 2002** East Bay Regional Park District fact sheet "Proposed 'Parks 2002' Ballot Measure, March 5, 2002."

125 **This time the measure enjoyed** *East Bay Express*, February 27, 2002.

125 **Again the measure garnered** League of Women Voters election results for March 5, 2002, from www.smartvoter.org.

125 **Though it had polled strongly** Exit Poll, Measure K, March 2002 Elections, Strategy Research Institute, March 2002.

125 **After the second defeat** O'Brien oral history, 2008–2009; author interview in 2009 with O'Brien.

125 **To the board's credit** League of Women Voters election results for November 2, 2004, from www.smartvoter.org.

## Chapter 10

127 **Due east of Mount Diablo (and pp. 92–93)** Author interview in 2009 with Bob Doyle.

129 **"That valley shows you . . ."** Pat O'Brien. "An Entrepreneur for the Environment: Creative Leadership of the East Bay Regional Park District and Four Decades in California's Local Park and Recreation Agencies, 1968–2008." Oral history interview conducted by Laura McCreery in 2008–2009. Bancroft Library.

130 **As William Penn Mott** William Penn Mott. "Dynamic Park Leadership, 1962–1967." Oral history interview conducted by Mimi Stein in 1981.

130 **One acquisition that took at least (and pp. 130–132)** O'Brien oral history, 2008–2009; author interview in 2009 with O'Brien.

132 **Under Rosemary Cameron's direction** Author interview in 2009 with Rosemary Cameron.

132 **Camp Arroyo's curriculum** O'Brien oral history, 2008–2009.

133 **The concept of environmental education** Author interview in 2009 with Ted Radke.

133 **In offering interpretive programs** Ron Russo. "Retired Chief of Interpretation, Recreation, and Aquatic Services." Oral history interview conducted by Edward MacKay in 2004.

133    **The District had always offered**   Author interviews in 2009 with O'Brien and Cameron.

133    **Elected to the board in 1994**   Author interview in 2009 with Carol Severin.

134    **In an early 2008 survey**   East Bay Regional Park District 2007–2008 Community Survey. Strategy Research Institute.

135    **"We borrowed from the corporate world …"**   O'Brien oral history, 2008–2009.

136    **Sutter, a retired judge**   Author interview in 2009 with John Sutter.

136    **Wieskamp, a veteran of local**   Author interview in 2009 with Ayn Wieskamp.

136    **Already a twenty-year veteran**   Author interview in 2009 with Radke.

137    **"Only if I have a dead body …"**   *San Francisco Chronicle*, January 21, 2006, p. B-4.

137    **Siri's sudden death**   Author interviews in 2009 with O'Brien and Radke.

137    **"She elevated the park district's concept …"**   **(and pp. 137–140)** O'Brien oral history, 2008–2009.

141    **In the late 1990s**   Author interviews in 2009 with O'Brien and Radke.

142    **The twenty-first century was well**   Author interview in 2009 with Doyle.

142    **"It was important to make it an extension …"**   Author interview in 2009 with Radke.

142    **"That figure took our breath …"**   Author interview in 2009 with Doug Siden.

143    **On July 1, 2008**   Approved Minutes, Regular Board Meeting of July 1, 2008.

143    **Having weathered the frantic run-up**   Author interview in 2009 with Radke.

143    **The first sign of trouble came (and pp. 143–146)** O'Brien oral history, 2008–2009; author interviews in 2009 with O'Brien and Jerry Kent.

146    **An exit poll analysis showed**   East Bay Regional Park District Measure WW. "Understanding Voter Behavior in the Face of a Unique Set of Challenges, November 2008." Strategy Research Institute, 2008.

### Epilogue

150    **The anniversary year proved the right time**   Author interviews in 2009 with Pat O'Brien, Rosemary Cameron, and Mike Anderson.

150    **In late October the land title**   Author interview in 2009 with Nancy Wenninger.

# Acknowledgments

This history of the East Bay Regional Park District owes its existence to two of the agency's administrators, Pat O'Brien, General Manager, and Rosemary Cameron, Assistant General Manager, Public Affairs. Although they commissioned the book to inform and engage a broad range of regional park users, supporters, and employees, they allowed me great freedom to propose and develop the story, never wavering in their support of my efforts. I thank them for an extraordinary collaboration.

Like any short book about a long topic, this work delves selectively into key events and turning points in order to characterize a more complex story. As an administrative history, it centers on those in positions of power, whether paid managers, legislators, or board members acting in a voluntary role to create, shape, and sustain the largest regional park agency in the nation. Others have told, and will continue to tell, the equally important story of individual parks and the dedicated employees and local volunteers who make them thrive. Because of the limited scope, readers may wish to seek out other histories and guidebooks about the regional parks and trails.

In my own research, I drew inspiration and primary-source material from Mimi Stein's series of oral history interviews of the early 1980s and the resulting book, *A Vision Achieved: Fifty Years of East Bay Regional Park District*, both carried out with a strong assist from Carole Hicke. Of the oral histories outside that series, Ann Lage's expert interview of David E. Pesonen stood out above all.

I gratefully acknowledge the District's fine board of directors. Although I worked most closely with Ted Radke, who increased my understanding of all things political and environmental, each of the other directors—Doug Siden, Beverly Lane, John Sutter, Carol Severin, Ayn Wieskamp, and Whitney Dotson—added greatly to this story. I also had the pleasure of talking with many former board members, and I especially applaud Jocelyn Combs, James H. Duncan, and the late William F. Jardin.

Although he retired as the District's assistant general manager in 2003, Jerry D. Kent supplied expert counsel time and again over many months. His firsthand knowledge of events was trumped only by his thoughtful consideration of their larger significance. Indeed, I often consulted others only to have them say, "What does Jerry think?" I am especially indebted to him for guidance on Chapters 5 ("Voters") and 8 ("Stewardship").

Over and above my frequent and essential consultation with Pat O'Brien and Rosemary Cameron, other District leaders played a valuable role in shaping this history. Bob Doyle, Assistant General Manager, Land Acquisition, generously shared his own story and discussed land-use politics. His early review of Chapters 3 ("Land") and 7 ("Shoreline") proved especially useful. I also warmly thank Assistant General Managers Mike Anderson, Tim Anderson, Dave Collins, John Escobar, and Ted Radosevich, each of whom was important to the narrative.

Many other staff members responded to questions and reviewed sections in draft (although I alone am responsible for any errors). I thank especially Stephen W. Edwards, director of the Regional Parks Botanic Garden; Brad Olson of the Resource Enhancement Program; supervisor Traci Parent at Black Diamond Mines Regional Preserve; trails manager Jim Townsend; land acquisition manager Nancy Wenninger; and retired supervisor Frances Heath and ranger Darrell Jones, both of Temescal Regional Recreation Area. At District headquarters, I had unfailing help from Mary Mattingly, Susan Rogers, Rosie Bock, Allen Pulido, and Shelly Lewis. Brenda Montano exceeded all requirements and expectations, skillfully locating and preparing photographs and archival materials over many months (with behind-the-scenes help from Isa Polt-Jones). Independent filmmaker Christopher Beaver, author of the splendid *After the Storm: Bob Walker and the East Bay Regional Park District,* navigated the Oakland Museum's collection of Walker's photographs, some 40,000 images in all, and recommended a selection of suitable illustrations to consider.

Although my ongoing oral history research at University of California, Berkeley's Institute of Governmental Studies stands apart from the writing of this book, my IGS affiliation amounted to valuable support and a certain symmetry as well: Samuel C. May, the first director of the Bureau of Public Administration—as IGS was then known—commissioned the Olmsted-Hall Report of 1930 and played a strong advocacy role in the District's formation in 1934. Seventy-five years later, I thank May's most recent successor, Director Jack Citrin, as well as Library Director Nick Robinson and his excellent staff.

I am grateful to those who so capably and collaboratively transformed the manuscript into a book: Roslyn Bullas, managing editor, and Laura Shauger, project editor, both of Wilderness Press, and Suzanne Albertson, book designer extraordinaire. Jason Armstrong kindly granted permission to use his photograph of Round Valley Regional Preserve on the cover.

With great appreciation, I acknowledge my personal sources of support and inspiration: Grete Cubie, Lynn Deetz, Brenda Jones and her family (Tom, Phoebe, and McLeod Sumner), Liese Karabetian, Germaine LaBerge, Ann Lage, Lauren Lassleben, Betty McCreery and the McCreery/Anderson clan, and especially Mary Ann Jones. My most profound gratitude goes to my husband, Bob McCreery, whose full heart and keen mind influenced every word of this volume.

# Photo Credits

Albert "Kayo" Harris: p. 10 (May 24, 1961)

Allan Mendez: p. 64 (2009)

Courtesy of The Bancroft Library, University of California, Berkeley, Johan Hagemeyer: p. 2 (1955)

Bob Walker, courtesy of the Oakland Museum: pp. 14 (1986), 33 (1989), 37 (1988), 52 (1987), 78 (1988), 82 (1987), and 91 (1988)

Brad Olson: p. 106 (top, 2004 and bottom, 2009)

Brad Polt-Jones: p. 133 (2007)

Brenda Montano: p. 76 (2009)

Brian Latta: p. 103 (2009)

Buck Joseph: p. 9 (1953)

Carl La Rue: p. 135, bottom (2008)

Cecil Davis: p. 11 (1963)

Citizens for Wildlife, Open Space, and Parks: p. 58 (1988)

Courtesy of Congressman Miller's Office: p. ix (2005)

Deane Little: pp. viii (2007), 26 (2008), 29, left (2007), and 35 (2008)

Direct Images: p. 146 (2009)

EBRPD file photos: pp. 6, 7 (both 1936), 8, top (1938), 8, bottom, 15 (1964), 16 (2004), 17 (1968), 18 (1973), 24 (2004), 28, 31, 63 (1988), 100 (2007), and 108 (2006)

Eric Nurse: p. 135, top (2004)

George Draper: p. v (2007)

Hillary Van Austen: p. 92 (2007)

Isa Polt-Jones: pp. 134 (2007) and 147 (2009)

J. A. Van Dis: p. 50, bottom (1979)

Jerry Ting: pp. vi (2009), 19, 29, 93 (all 2008), 124, and 148 (both 2009)

Joe Christianson: p. 38 (2008)

Kathleen Keilch: p. 131 (1999)

Kevin Fox: p. 152 (2008)

Laura Cottrell: p. 120 (2009)

Marc Crumpler: pp. 49, 94, and 126 (all 2008)

Mark Johnson: p. 110 (2009)

Nancy McKay: pp. 41 (1986), 42 (1985), 50, top (1985), 54 (1989), 62 (1992), 67 (1991), 84 (2003), 87 (1979), and 89 (1997)

Nancy Wenninger: p. 151 (2008)

Olmsted Brothers, Landscape Architects: p. xiv (1930)

Ralph Gray: p. 27 (1964)

Courtesy of Save the Bay: p. 80

Sean Duan: p. 140 (2009)

Shelly Lewis: pp. 13 (2006), 77 (2008), 85 (2007), 96 (2006), 99 (2008), 115 (2009), 117 (2007), and 143 (2005)

Steve W. Edwards: p. 105 (2007)

# Index

photos and photo captions  17, 50, 120

Proposition 13 and  21–23, 39–40, 50, 122

public safety and  21, 22, 50, 97–98

Tyler Ranch  151, 161, 162

Tyler Research Associates  40

## U

Udall, Stewart  18, 70

union. *See* labor union

University of California  1, 2, 3, 6, 10, 42, 72, 104, 107

Unruh, Jesse  79

Urban Care  87

Urban Land Institute  82

U.S. Geological Survey  103

Utah Construction and Mining Company  17

## V

Vail, Elbert M.  5, 6, 7–8, 74, 153, 154

Van der Ryn, Sim  46

Vasco Caves Regional Preserve  103, 117, 152, 160, 161

Vollmer, August  6, 153, 155

volunteers  108–109

## W

Walker, Robert "Bob" John  52, 58, 73, 186

Walpole, Richard  8, 9, 10, 153, 155

Warren, Earl  4, 6, 8

Waterbird Regional Preserve  101, 116

Weinberger, Caspar W.  80

Wenninger, Nancy  150

Western Electric  36

Wheeler, Douglas P.  88–89

Whitell Foundation  83

Wieskamp, Ayn  107, 108, 136, 139, 146, 149, 153

Wildcat Canyon Regional Park  32, 36, 159

Wildcat Canyon watershed  2, 6, 7, 104, 155

wildfire prevention and events. *See* fire prevention

Williams, Carroll  67, 74, 153

Wilson, Pete  88

Woolridge, Clyde  72, 153

Works Progress Administration (WPA)  4, 6, 7, 8, 77

## Y

Yemoto, Linda  133

## Z

Zierold, John  22–23